GUIDE TO STREAMING VIDEO ACQUISITIONS

ALA Editions purchases fund advocacy, awareness, and accreditation programs for library professionals worldwide.

AN ALCTS MONOGRAPH

GUIDE TO STREAMING VIDEO ACQUISITIONS

EDITED BY ERIC HARTNETT

CHICAGO 2019

ERIC HARTNETT is the director of electronic resources at Texas A&M University. His research runs the gamut of the electronic resource life cycle and covers such topics as trials, licensing, collection assessment and analysis, and resource management and maintenance.

© 2019 by the American Library Association

Extensive effort has gone into ensuring the reliability of the information in this book; however, the publisher makes no warranty, express or implied, with respect to the material contained herein.

ISBN: 978-0-8389-1766-4

Library of Congress Cataloging-in-Publication Data
Names: Hartnett, Eric, editor.
Title: Guide to streaming video acquisitions / edited by Eric Hartnett.
Description: Chicago : ALA Editions, an imprint of the American Library
    Association, 2019. | Series: An ALCTS monograph | Includes bibliographical
    references and index.
Identifiers: LCCN 2018015885 | ISBN 9780838917664 (paperback : alk. paper)
Subjects: LCSH: Libraries—Special collections—Streaming video. | Collection
    development (Libraries)
Classification: LCC Z692.S77 G85 2018 | DDC 025.2/873—dc23 LC record available at
    https://lccn.loc.gov/2018015885

Cover image © Adobe Stock.

⊗ This paper meets the requirements of ANSI/NISO Z39.48–1992 (Permanence of Paper).

Printed in the United States of America

23 22 21 20 19   5 4 3 2 1

CONTENTS

THE LIBRARY'S ROLE IN PROVIDING STREAMING VIDEO

Peter Shirts

While the purpose of this book is to address the logistics of providing streaming video for the library, it is important to begin with this introductory chapter on the need for and purpose of streaming videos in an academic setting. This chapter addresses two intertwined questions: (1) should libraries supply streaming videos? and (2) what do libraries' students and faculty want or expect, especially in an academic library setting, with regard to streaming video? While it might seem obvious that library users want access to as many streaming video titles as possible, current licensing models and constraints (budgetary, technological, etc.) on the acquisition of streaming videos suggest that an all-in approach may have some drawbacks for libraries in the short or long term. While individual cases may differ, balancing streaming video acquisition with more traditional physical video acquisition models may be a better approach for most libraries. This chapter presents evidence that favors this balanced approach, first discussing why libraries might use streaming videos, then highlighting some case studies that illustrate the increasing demand for streaming video, and finally finishing by looking at the ownership versus access debate that lies at the heart of video licensing.

PURPOSES OF STREAMING VIDEO

Why would a library want to invest in streaming videos? Its purposes may include (1) providing streaming videos for class use, (2) providing streaming videos for research, and (3) providing streaming videos for entertainment. These purposes categorize how and why library users consume videos, although unfortunately, any particular view instance or use can be hard to categorize (as is the case with traditional physical video circulation). The distinctions between these use categories become very important, however, once cost and frequency of use enter the equation. A short discussion of each of these categories follows.

Streaming Video for Class Use

While this topic will be covered adroitly by Mary Wahl in chapter 8, I will give a brief overview of streaming video in the classroom. Physical videos often work better for the in-class or viewing-session model because they are usually of higher quality, require less technical expertise, and avoid reliance on a possibly inconsistent Internet connection.[1] However, streaming video's popularity for class reserves is a result of (or perhaps a cause of) several important trends in education that are increasingly moving instruction outside of the classroom: (1) an increase in popularity of the flipped classroom approach, (2) an increase in distance education, and (3) the facility of streaming video to adapt for students with disabilities. Even outside of these increasingly common situations, teachers find that the ability of all of their students to both simultaneously and asynchronously watch a video outside of class is very appealing. Unless the video needs to be viewed in the shared experience of a classroom, many teachers and students now expect streaming video.

The impact of classroom streaming video on library collections is heavy video use for a few items, often with instructors using the same videos year after year. The many advantages of streaming videos for course reserves, along with the favorable cost-to-use ratio, make the acquisition of streaming videos a seemingly obvious choice, though only if acquisition is affordable (or available at all).[2]

Streaming Videos for Research

While high-use or popular videos are often used for research (for example, using a video as a primary source in film studies), frequently, the videos used for research are not the newest or most popular titles. Instead, researchers are using videos to get a glimpse of the past: how a locale used to look, how performances were staged, how topics were discussed, what artists looked like, and so on. These types of videos may receive little or no use year after year, but then suddenly they become very important. Research libraries may be the only institutions that are actually keeping and, hopefully, preserving these types of videos. Because streaming video licenses most often stipulate that libraries lose access to the video after the specified term is up, current streaming video models run counter to this type of research use, since low use does not justify the high price of streaming, and streaming services have a tendency to drop titles at any time, especially low-use titles. Some new streaming models, such as patron-driven acquisitions (PDA) programs (discussed at greater length in chapter 4), provide more affordable access to these low-use materials, though libraries cannot predict whether vendors will continue to maintain streaming access to particular low-use videos.

Streaming Videos for Entertainment

Library videos that are used mainly for entertainment can see medium to high circulation, with use usually tapering off as the material ages. These are the staple video type for many libraries. While public libraries have embraced entertainment as a primary purpose for video purchase, in an academic setting, support for this type of video use is still up for debate.[3] Many academic libraries see entertainment as an important reason for acquiring videos—for example, several years ago, two small academic libraries in the University of Hawaii system, UH-Hilo and Maui Community College, successfully promoted library use with a relatively cheap and popular DVD collection. But with the glut of popular streaming videos now available from services such as Amazon, Netflix, and Hulu, this promotional tactic may not work today. However, a 2014 study by Finlay, Johnson, and Behles found that popular DVDs that are also available on paid streaming services such as Netflix and Amazon were slightly *more* likely to be checked out from the University of Wisconsin-Whitewater library than those that were not on streaming services, perhaps because of their overall popularity (2014). This behavior could rapidly change, however—Morris and Currie found that 51 percent of surveyed library users at the University of Kansas stated they would rather pay $3 or less to view a film on a streaming service than come into the library to check out a DVD for free (2016). With many popular titles now available for institutional streaming licenses from services such as Swank Digital Campus and Hoopla, librarians have the opportunity to cater to the digital appetite, but at a hefty price. Ultimately, each library will need to decide if offering popular streaming videos is a good use of its resources if students can easily find these popular videos on ubiquitous streaming services.[4]

WHAT OUR USERS WANT

There is no question that physical video circulation has been declining in U.S. libraries. At the University of Hawaii at Manoa, the circulation of physical videos has decreased from over 100,000 checkouts per year at the peak in 2007 to under 10,000 in 2016. While this decline seems to be slowing, it does not appear to have bottomed out just yet. Meanwhile, more and more library users, especially in higher education, are accessing their video content via streaming—for example, in 2016 Netflix accounted for 70 percent of Internet traffic on campuses after 5:00 p.m. (Ferguson and Erdmann 2016). In 2016, the University of Hawaii at Manoa Library completed an IRB-approved online survey studying video use. Of the 180 students, mostly undergraduates, who responded to the survey, 82 percent had access to at least one commercial video streaming service, and 85 percent of those had access to Netflix streaming specifically; both of these numbers are higher than the national average, suggesting that college students are well ahead of the curve for streaming adoption. Not only did University of Hawaii at Manoa students have access to these streaming services, but they used them: 83 percent self-reported that they watched at least one hour of streaming video that week, and almost half (44 percent) of that subgroup reported watching more than five hours of streaming video that week. And despite the large collection of physical and streaming videos available from the library, 66 percent of respondents said they had never searched for a video in the library's catalog. In other words, in the new reality of streaming video ubiquity, the library has been mostly cut out of video distribution. Morris and Currie found remarkably similar results for student access to streaming services in a student survey at the University of Kansas (2016).

Faculty are showing the same preferences. While a few professors prefer to show the same VHS tapes they have used for twenty years, most faculty seem to prefer streaming video for their classes. Other librarians have remarked on this preference for streaming video at their respective institutions (Duncan and Peterson 2014; Morris and Currie 2016; Huddlestun 2017). As for using the library to provide streaming video resources, there seems to be a split—many faculty insist that the library provide these videos, while others find dealing with the paperwork, availability, and copyright issues too time-intensive and confusing and would prefer to find a free YouTube link or just not bother.

OWNERSHIP VS. ACCESS

As discussed above, libraries have good reasons to provide streaming videos to their users, whether for reserves, research, or entertainment, and students and teachers often want—and even expect—this service. But should libraries actually provide streaming videos? In many ways, the question of whether a library should acquire streaming videos or not boils down to the perennial debate about library ownership versus access.

On the ownership side, libraries want to control their own collections for (1) better preservation and (2) curation, or tailoring to users' needs. Preservation is a function that libraries provide as a service to society, one that libraries have by all accounts done more effectively than content creators and producers (Tsou and Vallier 2016); the desire to curate is one of the reasons why libraries continue to have local control and ownership of their materials.

Most streaming video models make ownership difficult, however, with consequences for preservation and curation—streaming videos are often not even available for libraries to purchase outright; a few may not even be available on physical media at all (Cross 2016). If streaming videos are available for ownership (often in the form of a "perpetual" license), most often the licenses are expensive—two to ten times the cost of those for physical videos—thus pricing these licenses out of the annual library funding model and forcing libraries to rely on yearly subscriptions. Furthermore, the library is often repaying for content that it has already purchased (for less money) in a physical format such as DVDs. Resource-sharing (such as interlibrary loan) for streaming videos, which is easy when libraries own items, is often impossible due to license restrictions (McGeary 2015). Streaming platforms commonly drop titles every year, which means that libraries cannot expect with certainty that a streaming video will persist in the future, even with a "perpetual" licensing promise.[5] Instead of librarians building collections based on the needs of their communities, the subscription model hands much collection-development decision-making to the vendors (King 2014). In the few cases when content providers allow streaming video preservation, this preservation adds additional expensive and time-consuming complications that are not encountered when preserving physical videos, and libraries are often not given significant compensation for this role as preservers of culture.

On the access side, streaming videos create easier access to the materials at any time or from any location that has Internet access—and while most students still have access to DVD players, an increasing number do not.[6] One question that is not often asked in this debate, however, is how accessible streaming video really is. Groups of library users exist who cannot access the infrastructure—an Internet connection fast enough, a device with a big enough screen—needed to watch streaming video, and while sometimes facilities can be provided that meet these needs, libraries cannot always ensure adequate facilities infrastructure, especially for distance education (Smith 2015). Finally, many videos are still only available on DVD or some other physical format, making total reliance on streaming video problematic (King 2014).

CONCLUSIONS

Streaming video is here to stay; the majority of our users expect its convenience and relative ease of use, and many will not even come into the library for a physical video anymore. However, the same users (who are used to accessing large commercial databases of streaming videos for one low, monthly price) often do not understand the heavy cost to libraries or the complicated nature of licensing—in most cases, streaming video subscriptions are far more costly than DVDs over the long term, without the benefits of ownership.[7] Libraries cannot turn their backs on streaming videos and risk losing relevance, but we should educate library users about the high cost of convenience, and we should advocate for the opportunity to preserve videos ourselves. Libraries, which are now in the midst of a serials crisis, should also think hard before they justify another expensive resource that needs to be paid on an annual basis and does not provide ownership. Libraries should lobby content creators, streaming providers, and lawmakers to create an environment in which libraries can own as well as distribute streaming media. In the meantime, for the sake of preservation and tailored collection-building, libraries should not completely abandon the acquisition of physical videos as they pursue streaming video acquisition.

Notes

1. We note that some teachers prefer the convenience of streaming videos, especially the ability to easily break up the videos into clips.
2. Furthermore, many students will not even watch an assigned DVD that is placed on reserve and held at the library.
3. The high cost of these streaming video platforms, combined with the limited availability of popular streaming services, shrinking library budgets, and the continued cheap cost of popular DVDs, means that physical video may still be the best option for public libraries.
4. University of Kansas libraries decided not to make a commitment to streaming for entertainment purposes, since many students already had access to platforms that provided these films (Morris and Currie 2016).
5. See King 2014. With perpetual preservation in mind, when a library is dealing with a streaming vendor, it should advocate for the streaming vendor to have both a perpetual option and a provision in the contract to hand over physical files for any streaming videos, should the vendor lose access or the company fold.
6. A 2016 survey of 180 students, mostly undergraduates, at the University of Hawaii at Manoa found that 17 percent did not have a way of playing a DVD at home, and 58 percent did not have a way of playing a Blu-ray Disc at home.
7. In a 2013 survey across all classifications of libraries, total spending on streaming videos exceeded spending on physical videos, and respondents indicated that they were planning on spending even more on streaming video in the coming year (farrelly and Hutchison 2014).

References

Cross, William. 2016. "More Than a House of Cards: Developing a Firm Foundation for Streaming Media and Consumer-Licensed Content in the Library." *Journal of Copyright in Education and Librarianship* 1 (1): 1–24. doi:10.17161/jcel.vlil.5919.

Duncan, Cheryl J., and Erika Day Peterson. 2014. *Creating a Streaming Video Collection for Your Library*. Lanham, MD: Rowman & Littlefield.

farrelly, deg, and Jane Hutchison. 2014. "Academic Library Streaming Video: Key Findings from the National Survey." *Against the Grain* 26 (5): 73–75.

Ferguson, Jennifer, and Annie Erdmann. 2016. "Streaming Video in Academic Libraries." *American Libraries,* September 21.

Finlay, S. Craig, Michael Johnson, and Cody Behles. 2014. "Streaming Availability and Library Circulation: An Exploratory Study." *LIBRES: Library & Information Science Research Electronic Journal* 24 (1): 1–10.

Huddlestun, Carey. 2017. "Tell Me What You Want: Material Format Preference of Music Faculty." Poster presentation, annual meeting of the Music Library Association, Orlando, Florida, February 22–26.

King, Rachel. 2014. "House of Cards: The Academic Library Media Center in the Era of Streaming Video." *The Serials Librarian* 67 (3): 289–306. doi:10.1080/036152 6X.2014.948699.

McGeary, Brian James. 2015. "Accessibility, Collaboration, and Staffing: Revamping the Model for Academic Library Video Collections." *Public Services Quarterly* 11 (November): 308–18. doi:10.1080/15228959.2015.1095672.

Morris, Sara E., and Lea H. Currie. 2016. "To Stream or Not to Stream?" *New Library World* 117 (May): 485–98. doi:10.1108/NLW-03-2016-0021.

Smith, Aaron. 2015. "U.S. Smartphone Use in 2015." Pew Research Center Report, April 1. www.pewinternet.org/2015/04/01/us-smartphone-use-in-2015.

Tsou, Judy, and John Vallier. 2016. "Ether Today, Gone Tomorrow: 21st Century Sound Recording Collection in Crisis." *Notes* 72 (March): 461–83. doi:10.1353/not.2016.0041.

WORKFLOWS

David Hellman

The *Oxford English Dictionary* defines workflow as "the sequence of industrial, administrative, or other processes through which a piece of work passes from initiation to completion; the passage of a piece of work through this sequence."[1] In libraries, workflow is often thought of as a particular series of components that make up a technical process, and often it is, but in this chapter we will approach the concept of workflow as an overarching and complete "beginning to end" process. We will briefly discuss technical workflows in managing streaming video content, but we will also talk about workflow processes before and after the more technical elements come into play. To provide an overview of the entire process, let us consider the following workflow graphic (figure 2.1)

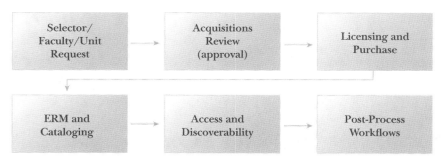

Figure 2.1 | **Workflow process**

SELECTOR, FACULTY, OR UNIT REQUEST

At many libraries, a request for a video typically comes in from teaching faculty for a particular title to be used in the classroom. Other institutions may want to have their library selectors build video collections to support the curriculum, or simply have streaming videos as one more resource to complement the entire collection. Unless a library's collection development policy designates particular subject areas that need coverage or there is suitable funding to integrate video selection with other monograph ordering, it is probably best to focus directly on curricular needs and allow the faculty's requests and classroom demand to drive video acquisitions. All formats present different challenges to workflow processes, and streaming video is no exception, but this format also presents certain advantages as well, including the obvious lack of a physical item that can be lost, damaged, and so on.

One way to automate the process is to create a web-based form and have users who are suggesting materials provide as much relevant information about the item requested as possible. By automating the process, you create a tool to gather necessary information and have the ability to pass that information along during the process. At a minimum, the requester should provide the following: requester's name, phone number, e-mail address, media title, year, price, vendor contact information, and where they saw it. In addition, for videos used in the classroom, ask for the department, class section/number, and the number of students enrolled in all the sections that will be using the video. On page 11 is a template for a potential form (figure 2.2).

Your Name *

Department *

Phone Number

Best number to reach you at. Include area code.

Email Address *

Confirmation email will be sent to this address.

For use in which course(s) *

Total Number of Students *

Media Title *

Year

Price $

Don't include the $. Numbers and decimal point only.

Where did you see it?

Additional Notes

Vendor Name

Vendor Email

Vendor Phone Number

Vendor Address

Figure 2.2 | **Video request form**

Alternatives to a web-based form can range from informal suggestions from faculty and other users to more formal approaches that are in line with established collection development policies, but with that said, a form offers the advantages of stability and uniformity that conform well with other parts of the workflow process.

ACQUISITIONS REVIEW (APPROVAL)

The review process can rely on a media specialist, individual subject selectors, a media review committee, or some combination of these. Whatever works best for the library and circumstances is the ideal way to proceed. At a minimum, the review should be aligned with whatever collection policies or guidelines currently exist or have been created for an emerging collection of streaming videos. The review workflow should include taking the information provided and vetting it. Is the requester affiliated with the institution and teaching the class(es) stated? Is the video offered by multiple vendors and other formats that can often provide savings? Does the request necessitate streaming video, or will other formats suffice? Will technical requirements exceed the technical infrastructure in place at the institution? Of particular importance is whether the video meets Americans with Disabilities Act (ADA) requirements and is accessible to disabled user populations (covered more thoroughly in chapter 9). These and potentially other questions need to be asked as part of the review workflow.

Libraries may also be subscribing to customized packages of streaming videos or comprehensive collections from vendors like Films Media Group, Alexander Street Press, or Swank. For these collections, a comprehensive collection review should be conducted to ensure the collection meets the needs of the campus and complies with ADA standards and other technical issues. Otherwise, the review workflow for these packages is relatively the same, with the major difference being that titles are processed in batches.

LICENSING AND PURCHASE

Once the review is complete, the licensing and purchase workflow is initiated. The appropriate vendor is contacted and a license is requested. An administrator, librarian, or staff member then reviews the license for the streaming video(s).

The license (covered in detail in chapter 5) should follow standard contract form, but one should pay particular attention to the details related to access to streaming content. Does the license provide perpetual access, or just access during a subscription term? Does cancellation require advance notice and if so, by what period of time? Does the license protect both parties without necessarily giving advantage to one over the other? A license for streaming content should be more or less the same as for any other electronic resource, but be sure that appropriate rights and entitlements are supported and guaranteed.

If the license is acceptable, an invoice is requested and then forwarded to the appropriate unit for payment. Typically, a librarian, collection development coordinator, or staff member will review the invoice. The terms and amounts should match anything agreed to during negotiations, and the net payment dates should be noted. Information from the invoice should be entered into an order record or an electronic resource management (ERM) system as necessary. When review of the invoice is completed, it should be forwarded to procurement, fiscal affairs, or other units that will process it for payment.

ERM AND CATALOGING

As part of the initial process, an order record should be prepared for the streaming video, and information and metadata should be added to an ERM system if the library uses one.

Now that the streaming video has been licensed and purchased, the vendor can be asked to provide MARC records. Vendors often provide MARC records, but if they are unavailable, try to access them through other means such as OCLC or, if that fails, proceed to an original cataloging effort. Before modifying MARC files, be sure to contact whoever handles authority control at the library. The best practice is to edit files at least one day before planning to upload them. Make sure the person in charge of authority control is aware of the plans and gives clearance when needed.

After downloading the MARC file(s), open it through a program such as MarcEdit. There are other programs available, but MarcEdit is recommended because it is free and relatively easy to use. Edit the fields as necessary. Fields that might need changing or updating are electronic location and access (856), local note (590), series added entry (830), local data (910), and in some instances, the control number for authority data (001). In addition, make sure the proxy prefix is added to the URL to ensure access (if licensed) remotely from the network. After modifying and inserting the fields, save the work. The modified file will need to be saved under the .mrc format in order to be uploaded into the library management system (LMS). Before doing that, be sure to test a couple of the URL links to make sure the files work. If the "proxied" URL leads to the source, then all is good. The records can now be uploaded into the catalog based on the established protocols the library is using. Note that standards and practices may vary depending on the particular software and LMS at the institution.

ACCESS AND DISCOVERABILITY

Now that MARC records have been edited and uploaded, the workflow process should be focused on managing other points of access and discoverability. At this stage, an electronic resources librarian or staff member with an appropriate level of expertise and experience will most likely handle the workflow responsibility. In terms of access, catalog records should be routinely checked for quality control and amended as necessary. For aggregated content, links and descriptions should be added to any appropriate database lists, research guides, or as news and "spotlight" items. Librarians and staff should be informed about the presence of new content, and subject specialists should likewise notify their constituents with regard to content that may be of interest to them. In terms of discoverability, content providers should be asked about the adequacy of indexing and coverage in major discovery services. If the library is using a particular discovery service, they can check to see if content is included in the portfolio of their resource knowledge base. Good discovery services should have decent coverage of most major electronic content, but it is important to verify the status of the particular content that is being added.

POST-PROCESS WORKFLOWS

Now that content has been selected, reviewed, licensed, and made available to users, there are other important additional workflows to consider that are essential for maintaining a stable and effective streaming video collection. The first consideration is scheduling regular maintenance of links. For individual titles that are acquired on a per-request basis, link stability should not be an issue, but for collections that are based on subscriptions, a regular scheduled review will be necessary. Most vendors both add and withdraw content on a semiannual basis, so it is good to know or be able to anticipate when these events will occur. It is important to establish proper protocols to ensure consistent access to licensed content, especially if it is related to assignments or used in classroom instruction. When lists of new content are received, they should be handled in a similar fashion to processes outlined in the ERM and cataloging section of this chapter. When content is lost, follow normal de-accessioning processes, but before that, review usage and identify heavily used titles which, if available, could be considered for individual licensing or purchase. A systematic approach to collecting usage data for electronic resources, preferably using a standard such as COUNTER, should be established and when possible stored in the ERM and disseminated as necessary. Finally, as with all collections, a regular weeding process is important for establishing reliable and useful content for users.

Now that multiple workflows in streaming video acquisitions have been reviewed, we will conclude by summarizing the main process in a workflow diagram (see figure 2.3 on page 16).

Note

1. "workflow, n.," *OED Online*, March 2017, Oxford University Press, www.oed.com. jpllnet.sfsu.edu/view/Entry/400203?redirectedFrom=workflow.

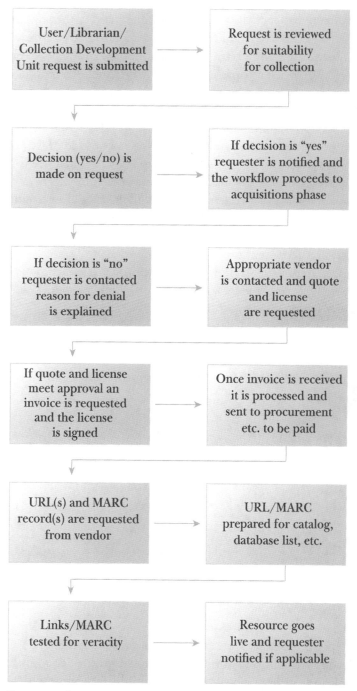

Figure 2.3 | **Streaming video workflow process**

COLLECTION DEVELOPMENT POLICY FOR STREAMING MEDIA

Planning for the Future of the Collection

Wil Weston

University collection development librarians often seem to worry about the strangest things; this is perhaps a function of the unique short-term and long-term planning that is an unceasing feature of all collection development work. Edelman (1979, 34) argues that collection development is simply a planning function of the library, and from the collection development plan flows the budget allocation. This does, generally, capture what may be considered the short-term aspect of collection development; simply, funds are allocated as effectively as possible to support the curricular and research needs of the institution. This is both an immediate and an annual challenge of funding the library's many subject areas at an appropriate level and, of course, the individual subject specialist's often-daunting task in selecting the content that a library needs for its subject areas of responsibility. However, collection development librarians are often most concerned with the long-term planning involved in their work.

Long-term planning is concerned with questions like: "What kind of collection are we building?" "Are we striking the right balance between access and ownership?" and "What will be the long-term effects of these short-term and often economics-driven decisions on the research collection as a whole?" This can be described as planning the overall shape of the collection and, in particular, trying to determine where its strengths and where its weaknesses are. The shape of the collection is not only the result of many short-term decisions, but the sum, the cumulative effect, of all the decisions that all of the previous collection development librarians have made during their tenures. In the past, this ongoing process of collection-building has been described in construction and assembly-like terms, such as building a bridge or a house. However, when looking at an institution's evolving curriculum and its new, emerging areas of research, the library research collection often feels more like a free-form spider web than a well-defined linear structure that is proceeding in some fixed, unchangeable direction.

The library collection, particularly at small- to medium-sized institutions, must evolve and change as the university evolves and changes. It is a near-constant struggle to tailor the collection to the research needs of its patrons while dealing with flat, stagnant, or shrinking collection budgets. New interdisciplinary programs, new areas of research, and an ever-changing faculty and student body should be reflected in what the library collects and how it provides access. However, meeting these new and evolving needs has been (and continues to be) complicated by a variety of issues such as new areas of study, new interdisciplinary areas of research, license agreements, and naturally, new formats.

Ultimately, the decision to add streaming videos to a collection touches upon many of these long-term concerns: new areas of research, curriculum changes, how patrons want to access content, and new license agreements. It is because of all of these complicated collection development issues that a collection development policy is necessary for streaming videos. This policy is a plan, or perhaps a blueprint, for how streaming videos will eventually impact the makeup of your library's current and future library collections.

THE CASE FOR A COLLECTION DEVELOPMENT POLICY FOR STREAMING VIDEOS

The purpose of any library collection development policy is to serve as a guide in the selection of materials to be added to the library collection, and the policy should highlight the strengths of the collection and identify those areas of lesser collecting interest. Additionally, the policy is used in the allocation of

collection funds across collecting areas. The ever-increasing cost of information acquisition, the rising demand for a variety of formats, and tightening
budgetary constraints now require very careful materials selection based on a
clearly articulated collection development policy.

Streaming videos are still relatively new, and there is keen interest on
the part of teaching faculty to use this streaming content in their courses
(Barlow, McCrory, and Blessing 2014). So, academic libraries need to address
this change in the faculty's teaching and research needs. However, in a recent
investigation, streaming media is notably not addressed in most collection
development policies (Morris and Currie 2016, 495). Guidelines relating to
streaming content can often be found on library websites and guides; yet,
the selection process for acquiring these materials and how content could be
streamed, and whether it is subscribed or purchased, was rarely addressed in
online collection development policies (Morris and Currie 2016, 495). And
it is critically important that the selection process be addressed. That process
is key to an understanding of the purpose of the library's collection; a collection development policy should answer why we "are" or "are not" collecting
in a subject area. However, in this case, the policy must also address how the
particular format of streaming video might ultimately impact the collection
that is being built for researchers. Again, it is the long-term planning that is
haunting the dreams of all those collection development librarians everywhere.

WHY STREAMING CONTENT FOR ACADEMIC LIBRARIES?

In just the last decade, streaming content (audio and video) has expanded and
significantly matured in consumer markets, particularly streaming videos for
television and movies. Also, there has been a considerable increase in the access
to both freely accessible and fee-based video materials. Currently, there are
numerous free, legitimate video sharing sites, academic publishers, nonprofit
archives, and, of course, commercial sites that offer streaming video content.
Furthermore, accompanying this increased growth in consumer markets and
growing academic streaming content, there has been a steadily growing interest
by teaching faculty in non-textual resources for instruction (DeCesare 2014, 5).

Video has always been a great supplemental resource for faculty; however,
now it is becoming more critical to their instruction and individual research
agendas (DeCesare 2014, 5). The idea of using auditory and visual methods

of presenting information to enhance the learning process for students is a well-established concept within current online learning pedagogy (Oliver 2000), and is rapidly becoming even more widely embraced by a growing audience of instructional practitioners. King (2014, 293) encapsulates this educational need for streaming by arguing that "film studies and media arts have become important disciplines over the past several decades; failing to provide for these classes would lead to the evisceration of important academic disciplines. Furthermore, the nature of contemporary university education requires robust access to non-print popular culture items. Interdisciplinary programs such as gender, area, and ethnic studies are almost unimaginable without access to these sorts of materials." Simply put, streaming content is a necessary format for instruction and is a necessary source of information for many disciplines, and it is one where a lack of access would simply mean that research and instruction in these areas would be difficult or even impossible to perform.

Finally, streaming options for content, like all electronic content, are very attractive to libraries that are facing space demands for new or expanding library services. How faculty are instructing students and the materials they use to teach are the primary drivers for these new library spaces. These new ways of teaching and learning mean that libraries cannot just have spaces where users sit in silence, are unable to work as a group, or cannot use mobile technologies (Childs, Matthews, and Walton 2016, 7). These library spaces are necessary for learning and are essential for an evolving information/media-literate student body. Streaming media offers a way to gain (and sometimes retain) space within the existing library building through the substitution of streaming content for physical media.

OKAY, STREAMING CONTENT IS NECESSARY; BUT HOW DO WE GET IT?

Although acquisitions and business models are more fully explored in chapter 4, there are a few acquisition details that collection librarians should be mindful of because acquiring streaming rights is an expensive and, frequently, a very time-consuming process. Generally, there are three models for acquiring streaming rights: purchasing the rights to digitize, purchasing the streaming rights, and leasing/purchasing a streaming collection (Duncan and Peterson 2014, 5). However, from a collection development perspective, though not always possible, the library should try to obtain perpetual rights to the streaming content when negotiating a purchase. Nevertheless, even if a library is unable to negotiate perpetual rights, sometimes perpetual access can be purchased on a title-by-title basis (Duncan and Peterson 2014, 5).

Additionally, there are now patron-driven acquisition (PDA) options for acquiring streaming video titles. Acquiring streaming videos through PDA is a natural evolution from the numerous PDA e-book options that are now available to academic libraries. This may in fact be a more appealing option due to the relatively low cost of leasing an individual title's streaming rights for a year versus having a year's subscription to a collection of streaming content. PDA, at a minimum, ensures that the library is only paying for access to items that have actually received use.

SIGNING ON THE DOTTED LINE

Licensing terms always need to be carefully considered by libraries because of their potential overall impact upon the library collection. Always review any language regarding Section 508 of the Rehabilitation Act and ADA compliance; in particular, the availability of closed captioning. Additionally, a quick review of the Libraries for Universal Accessibility website (http://uniaccessig.org/lua/vpat-repository) may be able to provide you with a Voluntary Product Accessibility Template (VPAT), which is a document that indicates if a particular library provider or publisher is in compliance with Section 508 accessibility guidelines. Accessibility is addressed in more detail in chapter 9.

Finally, look for any ambiguous language and unclear definitions of terminology; in particular, pay close attention to how "authorized users" is defined. There should never be any ambiguity in a license agreement, and while negotiating for access for your library, if something is unclear, ask for clarification and the inclusion of definitions (Duncan and Peterson 2014, 9).

WHAT ARE THE SELECTION CRITERIA OR BEST PRACTICES FOR SELECTING STREAMING CONTENT?

Inevitably, how a library selects material for inclusion in its collection will come up in conversations with subject specialists, who are selecting and recommending purchases, or with teaching faculty, who are recommending content to the library that they would like to be subscribed to or purchased. It is not recommended to add these criteria to the body of the collection development policy because criteria change; however, having them listed in the collection development policy's appendixes or online, as a separate document, where collection guidelines are discussed, is appropriate.

Generally, the recommended guidelines for the selection of streaming videos are similar to those for many other kinds of formats that libraries already subscribe to and purchase, like e-books and e-journals. For instance, relevancy to the curriculum, cost, and projected use of the content are ubiquitous across formats. Furthermore, as mentioned in the earlier section on licensing, it is important to be clear on the prohibited and permitted uses of the content—the vendor simply may not allow faculty or students to use the desired content in the way they wish. However, selection criteria that are unique to streaming videos might include the following: the authority of the filmmaker/distributor, the competency and consistency of the provider, the availability of content for immediate viewing, and how usage is determined.

The authority of the filmmaker/distributor is similar to the issue of publisher reputation and whether or not you are dealing with a predatory publisher. Moreover, as a selector, you have to be careful when applying this guideline, in particular for gender, ethnic, and area studies, where content from alternative and independent presses is critical. Additionally, it is a dimension which is continually being blurred by the growing ubiquity and sophistication of computer and video technology. As Greg Taylor (1999, 8) forecasted, "the special authority of the filmmaker seems an outdated notion: now anyone and everyone, it seems, can make movie art."

The competency and consistency of the provider are critical for a streaming service, specifically with regard to the authentication and stability of the content. Authentication seems to be less of an issue now than it was just a few years ago and is easily attributable to the "newness" of the format and working with academic libraries. But the stability of the online collection that is being subscribed to is critical for students and faculty who may want to use the content for teaching, study, or research. For example, with a subscribed streaming collection, content may be removed occasionally by the provider; if the provider decided to remove content without appropriate advance notification, then this will create problems for the teaching faculty using the online material in their classes. How the library is notified or how the notification is posted within the streaming service is key to the effective use of the streaming collection by faculty and students.

Finally, the availability of streaming content for immediate viewing and how that usage is determined are particularly important for PDA or demand-driven acquisition (DDA) streaming models. If there is any delay in access before the content can be viewed, or if there is additional authentication needed at the point of selection by the patron, there will be complaints, primarily because any delay in access will now likely not meet the users' experience or expectation of a streaming service such as Netflix, Hulu, or YouTube. It has long been known that any perceived convoluted checkout procedure, difficulty in navigation, or poor web performance will contribute to user dissatisfaction (Zhang and Von Dran 2001). Obviously, there are accelerated expectations associated with using any online service, but this is not surprising, since there is evidence that waiting in general will cause a user to negatively evaluate any service (Ryan, Pàmies, and Valverde 2015). If the built-in, environmental expectation is that access will be immediate, anything less than this will be considered as discouraging and a negative experience.

Also, how usage is determined is very important to understanding how a title might be triggered with a PDA/DDA product. It isn't just a matter of how many uses until a purchase is triggered; it is how a "use" is defined. How long can the video be watched before a purchase is triggered? What if it is the same user coming back to the same video? Do multiple views by the same user trigger a "use" each time the video is viewed? How the provider counts these individual uses matters because it will ultimately determine what the library is spending for access. It also matters, in the long term, for the library's assessment of the relative use and value offered by the streaming media product. However, always be careful when using this data because "use" data is likely to be counted differently from provider to provider. If a library is comparing streaming products, user feedback may ultimately be more valuable for assessment and selection purposes than "use" data.

CONCLUSION

The amount of streaming content and the number of providers for streaming content are only going to grow, as is the demand by faculty and students for more access. Currently, library budgets are strained to keep up with the rising cost of collections because of static funding levels. Furthermore, streaming content is often delivered as a service and is rarely offered with perpetual rights.

This, in the near term, may be immediately appealing to both libraries and users; however, streaming content delivered as a service is not adding to the collection. In the long term, how streaming content does or does not shape an academic library collection must be reflected in the library's collection development policy; it is the plan for the future of the collection.

Media will always be an important part of a research collection, and the balance between access and ownership is a compromise that will continually have to be negotiated annually. Collection development librarians must always keep the currently established research collection in mind when making their decisions on how that collection will be further developed and made accessible. The long story of collection decisions and material selections that have shaped and continue to shape an academic research collection serves to remind us all of the importance of our current collection development decisions. Streaming content is important. Streaming content has a place in the library collection and as a library service. However, its importance within each academic library must be carefully articulated in the collection development policy.

References

Barlow, Angela, Michael McCrory, and Stephen Blessing. 2014. "Classroom Observations and Reflections: Using Online Streaming Video as a Tool for Overcoming Barriers and Engaging in Critical Thinking." *Online Submission* 1: 238–58.

Childs, Sarah, Graham Matthews, and Graham Walton. 2016. "Space in the University Library: An Introduction." In *University Libraries and Space in the Digital World*, edited by Graham Matthews, 1–18. London: Routledge.

DeCesare, Julie A. 2014. *Streaming Video Resources for Teaching, Learning, and Research.* Chicago: American Library Association.

Duncan, Cheryl J., and Erika Day Peterson. 2014. *Creating a Streaming Video Collection for Your Library.* Lanham, MD: Rowman & Littlefield.

Edelman, Hendrik. 1979. "Selection Methodology in Academic Libraries." *Library Resources & Technical Services* 23 (1): 33–38.

King, Rachel. 2014. "House of Cards: The Academic Library Media Center in the Era of Streaming Video." *The Serials Librarian* 67 (3): 289–306.

Morris, Sara, and Lea Currie. 2016. "To Stream or Not to Stream?" *New Library World* 117 (7/8): 485–98.

Oliver, Ron. 2000. "Exploring Strategies for Online Teaching and Learning." *Distance Education* 20 (2): 240–54.

Ryan, Gerard, Maria del Mar Pàmies, and Mireia Valverde. 2015. "WWW = Wait, Wait, Wait: Emotional Reactions to Waiting on the Internet." *Journal of Electronic Commerce Research* 16 (4): 261–75.

Taylor, Greg. 1999. *Artists in the Audience: Cults, Camp, and American Film Criticism.* Princeton, NJ: Princeton University Press.

Zhang, Ping, and Gisela M. Von Dran. 2001. "User Expectations and Rankings of Quality Factors in Different Web Site Domains." *International Journal of Electronic Commerce* 6 (2): 9–33. www.jstor.org/stable/27751011.

4

BUSINESS MODELS FOR STREAMING VIDEO

John Ballestro

With demand for streaming video on the rise from undergraduate students to teaching faculty, library budgets are straining to meet the 24/7 need. Most libraries have shrinking budgets and weakening buying power, leaving acquisitions and media librarians the unenviable task of balancing and stretching the budget between print sources that remain popular and the explosion of streaming video, while still trying to maintain a balanced collection to meet or exceed their patrons' needs. At home, customers can easily access video services such as Netflix and Hulu with just a monthly fee. Incoming undergraduates grew up with these services and expect libraries to accommodate their viewing habits. However, academic libraries struggle to meet the demand, since vendors have much more complex business models and corresponding workflows to acquire streaming video. Because of the wide variety of vendors a library will communicate with to purchase streaming video, a library can expect the mode of delivery of content to be just as varied. Library technical staff and subject specialists must work in tandem to produce efficient workflows that will give their patrons quick and easy access to the content.

Not only do libraries struggle with the streaming medium; vendors, publishers, and even the content creators themselves grapple with how to make their content available and form pricing models that make the videos affordable for the widest audience while keeping an eye on their own bottom line (Schroeder and Williamsen 2011, 93). This, along with libraries' budget struggles, make the choices of how, when, and where to purchase streaming video difficult.

SINGLE-TITLE PURCHASING MODEL

Business Model: Purchasing Single Titles for X Number of Years

To preface a library's buying options, a library needs to realize that most vendors do not have an in-perpetuity model. Libraries are purchasing streaming videos like they do databases; they are leasing access to the content. Even most publishers that allow licensing in perpetuity stipulate that it is only for the life of the file. As Lerner explains, digital-born files only have a shelf life of ten to fifteen years because the software that is used to read the code changes, so often the files become out of date, making older versions harder to read and ultimately obsolete. This makes digital files more fragile than their physical counterparts (Lerner 2001, 174).

When Texas A&M University (TAMU) Libraries started looking for and purchasing streaming videos, the business model of purchasing single titles was the most prominent one. This model basically consists of purchasing a single title for X number of years. During this time, aggregators had not started building their databases, and libraries were working mostly with smaller vendors or even the rights holders themselves, who did not have their own platform to stream their content. Today, libraries have much wider options of business models to choose from. However, unlike e-books, where a title can be sold through multiple platforms, giving the library the options of several modes of digital rights management (DRM) and visual platforms, a streaming title is generally held by one vendor, on one platform. Rights holders can choose to sell directly to libraries, giving them the right to stream on their own local server or work with another company to sell their content; again, either to stream locally or on the vendor's platform.

The model of purchasing title by title allows for the greatest control by the library. The library knows exactly which title it is purchasing for X amount of dollars for X number of years. Vendors generally work on a one-year, three-year, give-year, or "in perpetuity" pricing and licensing scale. Purchasing title by title generally costs more per title; some vendors work with a flat fee per title for every library, while others install the tier pricing based on the full-time equivalent of the entire university or even the number of students in the class to which the content will be streamed. But having said this, title-by-title purchasing is the only model that allows for true ownership of the title by negotiating for streaming in perpetuity or the life of the file (Handman 2010, 330). Another plus for libraries in this model is the ability to make a copy for preservation purposes. This can be negotiated in the licensing process if the library is purchasing a physical copy along with the streaming rights.

Mode of content: As a library works through this business model, staff must be aware that they will be working with the widest variety of vendors. Library staff could be working with a single person who has never worked with a library to license or sell his or her content. Since the types of vendors and rights holders are so different in this model, the mode in which we receive the content is also the most varied. Over the past five years, TAMU has purchased hundreds of titles on an individual basis and has received the content in these ways:

- A physical piece (DVD) that the library must digitize and place on its own password-protected server. Copyright must be adhered to in this step
- Files in several formats sent to the library on a flash drive to be placed on the library's server
- Files placed on the vendor's FTP server that the library downloads to a local computer and then works to place it on the protected server
- Files sent through e-mail as an attachment
- Streaming content hosted on the vendor's platform

A library must keep these various methods in mind when working with smaller vendors or individuals. A majority of these modes have the library performing extra steps in order to make the content accessible to its patrons. Properly allocating staff for licensing, purchasing, and digitizing can make the process much more efficient.

MARC records: For this business model, most individuals or smaller vendors do not provide MARC records. However, if you are purchasing from an established vendor that hosts the content, a library can usually retrieve MARC records from an administrative portal through the vendor's website.

SUBSCRIPTION-BASED MODELS

Business Model: Subscription-Based

Another business model that libraries will encounter when purchasing streaming video is the subscription model. This vendor-hosted model acts like a serial subscription, with a licensed time frame and generally a lower cost per title. Farrelly and Hutchison (2014, 74), in his survey of academic libraries, notes that "subscription video collections account for the largest portion of library spending on streaming video." Because this model acts similarly to a journal package subscription, at the end of the contract or subscription date, a renewal will need to be agreed upon by both parties. At that time, just as with journal titles that move in and out of the package, streaming titles within the package may no longer be available and the library will lose access to that content. These subscriptions work more like an e-book set where the title list is fluid and as content moves out, a vendor may replace the content with other content that they believe is just as desirable as the content that moved out. The difference between serial and streaming video subscriptions is that with most serial packages, even if a library cancels the subscription, it can negotiate up-front that it retains access to the content years that it has already purchased. However, once a library cancels a streaming video subscription, all access and content are lost permanently.

As with any package, the advantage of a subscription model is the number of titles the library is offered. Subscriptions allow for financial flexibility during times when the library's budget is tested. A drawback to subscriptions and packages is that a library will have low and even no views or usage on a higher percentage of videos. Assessment of the usage is thus key to determining if the return on the investment is worth renewing for future years.

Mode of content: The subscription model is hosted on the vendor's or a third-party platform using a form of patron authentication for access.

MARC records: Add/Delete MARC records are generally provided in this model. TAMU has seen one vendor provide one large file with X amount of records in it, and another vendor provide a zip file containing as many as 20,000 individual files (one file per title). Staff time for record maintenance of titles moving in and out will need to be devoted to these subscriptions.

Business Model: One-Time Package Purchase Model

Though it is related to the subscription model, the one-time package purchase model has several differences: price, stability, and length of access. As with the subscription model, package purchases can have any number of titles and are usually theme-based. The themes could be a package of publisher titles, subject-based, time periods, and even profession-based. Dance, theater, World War II, clinical patient interviews, and silent films are just a few of the types of packages a library could consider.

With one-time purchases, a library should expect the pricing to be significantly higher than a subscription-based package. The advantage with the one-time purchase model is that the library gains perpetual access to these titles, and the titles in these packages are relatively stable. Titles rarely move in and out of the group, so the library does not have to spend as much time with the maintenance of the package. Generally, vendors are adding content, or finishing up the promised title list, as the year progresses.

A library may see high use for several titles and little to no use on other titles within the package.

Mode of content: The one-time model is vendor-hosted on their or a third-party platform using a form of patron authentication for access.

MARC records: Add/Delete MARC records are generally provided in this model. However, these sets are generally stable, and staff time for record maintenance of titles moving in and out should not be burdensome.

ON-DEMAND MODELS

Business Model: PDA/DDA

The often synonymous duo of patron-driven acquisitions (PDA) and demand-driven acquisitions (DDA) will not be separated in this chapter. Both models engage the library's patrons in the collection development process as libraries increasingly adopt "just in time" models of purchasing (Aroughetti 2017). With this model, libraries work with vendors to choose a set of titles that will be accessible for their patrons to view. The title list could be the vendor's entire database, or a customized set of titles that mirrors and enhances the library's current collection development policies. Vendors can also make sure that any titles a library may already have access to via another supplier can be taken out of the PDA database.

Typically, a vendor will ask for a minimum payment up-front to deposit into the PDA account. Library staff will have to determine how much their budget can handle, and this may affect the number of titles at the start. If the library is unsure how fast the deposit will be depleted, it can always start with smaller amounts (or the minimum a vendor requires) and work through that deposit, noting how long each deposit lasts. Once the minimum is spent, a library is no longer required to continue with the PDA program. This is where the flexibility comes into play. The library controls the money, understands how much it can spend, and once that amount is spent, the library can make an assessment and decide to either continue the program with another deposit or put the program on hold.

Once the PDA database is in place and access is turned on for those titles, the vendor monitors the usage of each title. Once a title is viewed a certain number of times or for a certain number of minutes (or a combination of the two, depending on the vendor's matrix), the title is triggered for purchase. The cost of the title is taken from the deposit. In the two PDA programs TAMU participates in, the license or term of access for a triggered title is one year. Once a year passes, the title then reverts back into the PDA pool and can be triggered again. If the library sees that a title is being triggered year after year, vendors may offer a discounted price on multiple-year licensing, and if this is accepted by the library, the title is then taken out of the PDA pool.

One of the unexpected advantages that a PDA program has over title-by-title purchasing is the reduction of staff time dedicated to individual licensing.

With a PDA program, a library negotiates one license up-front and the terms cover the entire database. So if twenty-five titles are triggered during a calendar year, no other licensing is needed. From FY14 to FY16, TAMU saw a sizable increase in the number of licenses that staff had to negotiate (see figure 4.1). Near the end of FY16, TAMU initiated two PDA programs. Both

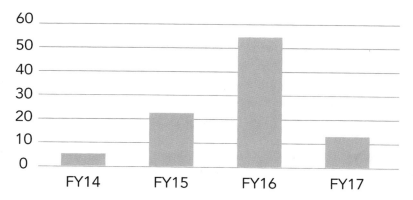

Figure 4.1 | **Streaming licenses per fiscal year**

programs were large (more than 15,000 titles in each one) and greatly reduced the number of licenses that staff had to negotiate the subsequent year (FY17). This has saved a tremendous amount of staff time and paperwork and has brought our level of licensing down to that prior to FY15. Another advantage is knowing that each title which is triggered for purchase has had some use, so the cost per use is much lower than in other business models.

A disadvantage to the PDA program is that titles can move in and out of the database without much warning or explanation. Vendors will send monthly updates through informational e-mails describing the new additions, but they will also give warnings of titles that they no longer have the rights to stream. In these cases, a title already triggered for purchase will not become inaccessible. Once the licensing term is up for that title, it will not go back into the PDA pool. However, it may still be available to purchase individually from the same vendor. Another disadvantage is that not all of the vendor's titles or packages are available for PDA.

Mode of content: PDA models must be on a vendor's platform in order for that vendor to keep track of usage, licensing, and triggered titles.

MARC records: Add/Delete MARC records are generally provided in this model. TAMU has seen one vendor provide one large file with X amount of records in it, and another vendor provide a zip file that contains as many as 20,000 individual files (one file per title). Staff time for record maintenance of titles moving in and out will need to be devoted to the PDA model.

EVIDENCE-BASED MODEL

Business Model: Evidence-Based Model/Access to Own

One of the newer models for libraries to choose from is the evidence-based acquisition (EBA) model. This model is also used in e-book packages, and is an offshoot of the patron-driven acquisitions model. The titles used in this model have a mediated title list that is agreed upon between the vendor and the library. The library can choose certain packages or years within a package that the vendor has to offer. The package can be based upon subject areas, genres of movies, or even one to multiple production companies. At the same time, the library and vendor agree upon the length of time for the program and how much the library will need to pay up-front before access is turned on. Once the title list has been set, the library is granted full and unlimited access to these titles. After the agreed-on time frame has lapsed, the vendor gives the library usage data for the package. The library can then decide which titles to receive discounts on or get permanent access to (depending on the deal struck between the two parties) until the prepayment runs out.

The advantages of this model are the usage data given to the library so that it can make an informed decision on which titles to own or license for X number of years. The library does not have to choose the top-used titles, but can assess the data to become informed about patrons' viewing habits. Librarians can build a more cohesive collection with this data. Another advantage is the stability of the title list. Once the list is confirmed between the vendor and the library, it is very rare that a title is taken out of the title list.

The disadvantage is that the prepayment can be quite hefty, so the minimum spend is larger than in a patron-driven acquisitions model.

Mode of content: Evidence-based models have to be on a vendor's platform in order for the vendor to keep track of usage.

MARC records: These packages have a set amount of titles that do not move in or out of the package, so there is a one-time file transfer of MARC records, generally through OCLC or an FTP server.

USE-BASED MODELS

Business Model: Pay per View/Circulation

The pay per view model mimics transaction-based models such as Amazon and DirecTV. It allows a library and vendor to coordinate a database of titles that can either be static, or which changes as movies are released for streaming and are added to the database. Authenticated patrons browse titles through a content provider's platform and decide on the spot which title to start streaming. The cost to the library ranges from $0.99 to $4.99 per title depending on the episode, show, or movie (Enis 2013). While mostly geared to public libraries, two types of pay per view models have emerged: one where the patron downloads and can view the movie for a specific amount of time on a mobile device or PC, and the other where the patron is limited to viewing the movie streamed on the vendor's platform and is not able to download the content to a device. In both versions, there is no permanent ownership of the material by the library. However, the cost per transaction is generally lower, the library can cap the number of streams or downloads per week or per month, and usually there aren't any platform or subscription fees.

Libraries can work with vendors on the number of patrons that are allowed to download or stream the movie at the same time. And by setting a monthly allowance, libraries can monitor usage and monies spent. If there is any money left over at the end of the month, vendors allow the money to be reallocated to the next usage period.

Mode of content: Content is browsed through the vendor's platform. The streaming video can either be streamed on the platform or be downloaded to a device, depending on the vendor.

MARC records: MARC records are provided. Staff time will need to be devoted to the maintenance of the files, since titles are added and deleted on a monthly to quarterly basis.

UNAVAILABLE

Business Model: No Streaming Access

As streaming videos become more integrated with professors' curricula, a library can come across a request for a title that simply can't be streamed. Whether the driving force is that the rights holder cannot be contacted, the distributor or director simply does not want their content streamed, or a vendor does not want to license that streamed content to an academic library, the purchasing library and, in turn, the requesting professor or patron need to be aware that some titles can't be viewed via streaming, and so they may have to resort to using the library's hard copy.

With regard to libraries, services such as Hulu, Netflix, and Amazon are now creating their own content, but sometimes (1) they are not offering streaming services for libraries, and (2) they are also not offering their shows in a hard-copy format (Blu-ray/DVD). When this is the case, frustration mounts for patrons who want to view, discuss, and research that content. Netflix has started to open up its original documentary content through a limited one-time-only viewing of its documentaries (https://help.netflix.com/en/node/57695), but that is a very small percentage of content available for a limited duration, and it may only be accessed via the Netflix service by a Netflix account holder. Thus, there will be times when library staff have to tell their patrons that content is simply unavailable to stream, or they must even purchase a hard copy.

WHAT QUESTIONS TO ASK?

When deciding which of the models described above is best suited for your library, there are certain questions that you'll need to ask before jumping into the fray.

How Do I Start with X Amount of Money?

As farrelly puts it, 49 percent of libraries that are currently purchasing streaming videos say the funds come from their general library budget. This means that there aren't any extra funds carved out for this content (farrelly and Hutchison 2014, 74). First, you should determine if the funds you are going to use are a one-time surplus or will be coming from your base budget year after year. If you have just one-time funds to work with, PDA and evidence-based models allow for this. PDA, even for a year, gives you some idea of the types of videos your patrons use. Evidence-based models do the same thing, but with a mediated collection development layer that is determined at the beginning of the process. Subscription models get you access to the most titles per dollar, but most vendors would want more than a one-year commitment from the library. If you want to be more focused in your collection development, then title-by-title purchasing allows control over the monies, along with a higher chance that your library can own the title. TAMU currently has a "Suggest a Purchase" link on its website where patrons can suggest content for their research needs; this includes DVD, CDs, and streaming video requests from faculty. This type of hybrid PDA portal gives patrons the ability to request something, and it gives the library the chance to consider an item that most likely will be used at least once in the future.

How Much Should I Put Down for a PDA- or Evidence-Based Model?

The evidence-based model is largely based on vendor pricing, and you may be able to negotiate a price you are comfortable paying. Pricing depends on how large the title list is going to be. The more titles, the larger the year range, and the more production companies, the higher the price the vendor will ask because all of the content is fully accessible during that time. This model will have the largest up-front commitment.

For PDA, the pricing depends on how long you want the access to last and the type of institution you work in. For example, TAMU, being a heavy STEM (science, technology, engineering, mathematics) school, might not spend as much in a PDA model in the same amount of time as a smaller liberal arts school that has a strong cinema or theater curriculum. There is usually a small minimum payment, but for your first venture into PDA, you can always try the minimum, see how long that lasts, and extrapolate that amount to a full year.

What If I Can't Find If a Movie Is Available via Streaming?

One resource to find streaming movies is the VideoLib discussion list (www. lib.berkeley.edu/MRC/vrtlists.html). This list hosts some of the film and media experts both in librarianship and on the business side of video content. Copyright, licensing, philosophical discussions, and even suggestions on where to find content creators are on this discussion list. Also, some vendors have a service to contact them (if you are a current customer), and they will devote resources to searching for the rights holder and will license the ability to stream the content on their platform.

CONCLUSION

Libraries have much to be concerned about regarding the rapidly growing popularity of streaming videos as vendors and content creators mold business models that affect not only how our patrons view the material, but also affect our libraries' resources, workflows, and particularly budgets. Which streaming business model a library chooses for its patrons depends on the type of funds a library has on hand, the staffing it has to handle maintenance, and the technology it has to digitize and host some of the content. Carefully considering all of these factors will help a library discover what the right model is for it.

References

Aroughetti, Stephen. 2017. "Keeping Up with . . . Patron Driven Acquisitions." Keeping Up with . . ., Association of College & Research Libraries. www.ala.org/acrl/publications/keeping_up_with/pda.

Enis, Matt. 2013. "More Vendors Help Libraries Stream Video." The Digital Shift. www.thedigitalshift.com/2013/07/media/more-vendors-help-libraries-stream-video.

farrelly, deg, and Jane Hutchison. 2014. "Academic Library Streaming Video: Key Findings from the National Survey." *Against the Grain* 26 (5): 73-75.

Handman, Gary. 2010. "License to Look: Evolving Models for Library Acquisition and Access." *Library Trends* 58 (3): 324-33.

Lerner, A. 2001. "Business Archives and Digital Images: Preservation Issues versus Getting the Job Out." *Imaging Science Journal* 49: 171-75.

Schroeder, Rebecca, and Julie Williamsen. 2011. "Streaming Video: The Collaborative Convergence of Technical Services, Collection Development, and Information Technology in the Academic Library." *Collection Management* 36: 89-106.

LICENSING STREAMING VIDEO

Erin DeWitt Miller, Sue Parks, and Andrew Trantham

A study in 2015 found that 68 percent of college students access and make use of streaming videos during their academic work requirements, and 79 percent use videos to supplement their coursework through further learning (Leonard 2015). Additionally, developments like blended learning and the availability of online courses and degree programs have increased the demand for online content (King 2014). Providing streaming video to support these needs involves licensing content, and with that come the various challenges inherent in the process of licensing any materials for library collections. This chapter will detail some of these licensing challenges and provide information that can be helpful for overcoming them, including an explanation of the types of licenses available, descriptions of specific contractual language that librarians should be aware of, and a few details about workflows. However, first it may be helpful to look at the ways that licensing streaming video has changed in the years since its beginning.

EARLY LICENSES

The *Guide to Video Acquisitions in Libraries* made note of several of the early barriers that existed in its observation that "there is no industry standard for licensing digital video, and many factors such as obtaining digital rights and tracking rights holders, identifying and meeting various institutional needs, and pricing models vary widely among vendors" (Laskowski 2011). While some of these issues continue to be challenges today, they presented unique problems in the early years of licensing online content. As noted in the introductory chapter, many libraries began licensing online content in response to the increased availability of online courses with video elements, and the subsequent demand by faculty and students to make this content easily accessible. Distributors of educational content were initially reluctant to discuss digitization and online delivery, fearing their content would no longer be protected and that users would download, copy, or share links. Distributors also shared concerns regarding the inability to license video for streaming due to complications with existing filmmaker agreements, where altering the format of the content was an exclusive right of the copyright holder and where distribution term limits dictated the availability of titles and content. Filmmakers and distributors also expressed concern with third-party content that required additional permissions and clearances not previously secured.

Initially, there were no license agreement templates to follow, and negotiations included discussing format types, delivery platforms, "life of file" issues, and methods of restricting access only to students enrolled in a particular course. Licenses for streaming videos were not viewed as standard electronic resource licenses, and so negotiating, managing, and executing their terms and conditions were often left to the media librarian. This resulted in the development of workflows and processes that differed significantly from those used for license agreements that were negotiated and managed by individuals and departments with greater licensing experience. Additionally, there were no vendor-developed delivery platforms, so individual institutions had to deal with the burden of digitizing and hosting content. Institutions were also required to have the necessary resources and infrastructure to support their own streaming video collections, which included setting up and maintaining servers, and having the ability to manage and limit access. This is likely the primary reason why vendors and institutions were initially slow to license and deliver streaming video content, and this process did not become more mainstream until vendors developed their own access and delivery portals.

GENERAL LICENSING LANGUAGE

With regard to streaming video licensing in the present, it might be surprising to some to learn that the general structure and vast majority of legal and business requirements for streaming video license agreements are very similar to those of any other license agreement or institutional contract. In fact, streaming video licenses tend to be much less complicated than standard license agreements for other types of electronic resources. The only truly unique language contained in streaming video licenses is found in their Grant of License clauses, which set out the legal parameters of the digitization and streaming process. A detailed example of a Grant of License clause from a streaming video license agreement is shown below:

> The LICENSOR hereby grants to the LICENSEE a non-exclusive license to digitize the LICENSOR's program, "Title of Video" (the "PROGRAM") from the DVD of the PROGRAM on the LICENSEE's digital network for streaming to the LICENSEE's faculty, staff, and currently enrolled students only. In addition, the LICENSEE agrees that the content of the PROGRAM shall be password-protected and that it will take all reasonable measures to protect the producers of the PROGRAM's rights under U.S. copyright laws. Such measures shall include warnings about copyright infringement when accessing the LICENSEE's digital network.

The language of this particular example (1) allows the institution to digitize the licensor's material from a DVD and host it on a local network; (2) restricts access to this digitized material to faculty, staff, and enrolled students; and (3) requires that the digitized material be password-protected. These provisions grant all of the necessary rights for an institution to host and provide access to streaming video for its users.

It is important to note that apart from their Grant of License clauses, streaming video license agreements are not particularly unique: they simply deal with specialized products and a few specialized rights. All the other language in streaming video licenses (Restrictions on Use clauses, Term and Termination clauses, Limitation of Warranty/Liability clauses, Governing Law/Venue clauses, Indemnification clauses, etc.) can be found in any electronic resource license agreement.

Consequently, streaming video license agreements need to conform to the same legal contracting requirements as any other license agreement. For example, many public institutions are bound by state statutes regarding indemnification, governing law, legal venue, and confidentiality. Any clauses that are known to be potentially problematic in streaming video license agreements should be carefully reviewed for legal compliance. If the language contained in such clauses does not comply with the institution's legal requirements, then the terms must be negotiated with the vendor. For this negotiation process, it is vital for libraries to have a strong awareness of their institution's legal contracting requirements, as well as a strong working relationship with their institution's legal counsel.

Some institutions also request or require Voluntary Product Accessibility Templates (VPATs) for all new electronic resources, including video products. VPATs are documents that explain in detail how electronic products do or do not comply with the accessibility requirements of federal law, specifically those found in Section 508 of the Rehabilitation Act of 1973. At present, the use of VPATs for video products is still relatively new, and the requirements at individual institutions vary widely.

CONSIDERATIONS FOR STREAMING VIDEO

In addition to the standard legal and business contracting requirements, there are a number of other factors to consider when licensing streaming videos. Practical considerations such as the hosting method and, of course, pricing can influence whether or not a streaming video license agreement will meet the needs of an institution. A large percentage of streaming video is now hosted on vendor-developed platforms. Many vendors do not require a separate license for each video, but will instead allow one overarching contract to cover all content as it is licensed. Titles licensed from smaller distributors generally require that an institution either have an in-house server and platform, or pay to host one-off titles on a vendor platform (Alexander Street Press, Kanopy, and others provide this option). The pricing for streaming video varies widely depending on the length of the license term and the size of the package purchased (some vendors provide a discount for bulk orders). It should also be noted that streaming video invoices sometimes contain language specifying terms and conditions that act as a license agreement, and any such language needs to be carefully scrutinized to make sure that it is legally compliant, and that it accurately reflects an institution's product expectations. The language in an invoice or contract that relates to the length of the license term, the breadth of user access, whether or not a public performance rights license is included, or that defines either perpetual access or archival rights, is especially critical to consider.

Term of the License

The length of the license term determines the period in which an institution can legally provide online access to a video. The most commonly available terms are one-year, three-year, five-year, and in perpetuity (the latter is commonly referred to as life-of-file, life-of-format, and perpetual access). Although it seems that the obvious choice for all streaming video acquisitions would be perpetual access, it is important to note that a large percentage of streaming video is not available to license in perpetuity. Additionally, whether a library's collection development policy emphasizes a just-in-case (permanent collection-building) or just-in-time philosophy (provision of access) should be considered. If the primary focus of collection development is ensuring that students can access a film in order to fulfill a course requirement, it may not be worth the expense of buying perpetual rights. However, in either case, if perpetual access is available for a similar price, then it will most likely always be the preferred choice.

When the duration of a streaming video license is limited, most agreements will define this period in simple and straightforward language. For example, "Subscription term is 12 months, starting on the date of the subscription invoice," or "The term of this Agreement shall commence on [date] and continue through [date] (the License Period)." It is always important to check the dates listed on a contract and ensure that they match the dates of access, especially if the process of invoicing and payment takes longer than expected and access is delayed. Because the concept of perpetual access is dependent upon formats and file types that will inevitably become obsolete, these terms should be very clearly defined (Duncan and Peterson 2014). Unfortunately, the current language defining perpetual access is frequently unclear or inadequate. For example, "X Institution is hereby granted the following licenses for digital streaming: Asynchronous digital streaming for the life of the format." The phrase "life of the format" could create unnecessary ambiguity in the future when libraries will have to determine how to proceed after a digital file format becomes obsolete.

Access Limitations

Another important factor to consider when licensing streaming video is the breadth of access provided to users; this language in a contract should be unambiguous. For most academic libraries, the preferred access will be a site-wide or institution-wide license that allows all affiliated faculty and students to access the streaming video. This level of access is typical for packages that include a large quantity of streaming videos such as those from Kanopy, Alexander Street Press, or Films on Demand. Usually, site-wide access is provided through IP or proxy authentication and is available for video collections regardless of the term length. An example of concise language that clearly allows for site-wide access is given below. Note that even in collections of material available to an entire institution, some content may be geographically restricted:

> "Authorized Users" means Institution's currently enrolled students, employees, faculty, staff, affiliated researchers, distance learners, authorized attendees at educational classes hosted by the Institution, and visiting scholars authorized to view the Product(s) and Institution Content including by remote access through an authentication (proxy) server that guarantees access only by Authorized Users. Certain Products (e.g. Hollywood titles) may have Territory restrictions on viewership, in which case these restrictions will be made known to the Institution at the time of purchase in the Order.

Small distributors, vendors of the rights to feature films, and niche market vendors such as those developing content for professionals will sometimes limit online access to a specific number or group of students such as those enrolled in a course. If content is hosted on the distributor's platform, this can be accomplished by simply not adding the licensed content to the public access catalog and only permitting the link to be shared through course software that requires individual authentication. If this content is digitized and hosted by the institution, it is necessary to ensure that the platform used for hosting includes a feature that allows content to be restricted to a course-specific log-in.

The copyright holders for a video are often the creators, their estate, or the original studio. It is becoming more common for distributors to negotiate the option of a perpetual license with the copyright holders, but it is still important to have the granted rights in writing for future reference in case of a dispute. Additionally, some license agreements require that specific language be included within a streaming video warning, such as "The Copyright Act forbids copying without permission from the copyright owner." License agreements may also specify that only one file type (such as an MP4) may be used to provide digital access, and some licenses even go so far as to require that the file be obtained directly from the distributor, rather than allowing it to be ripped from a DVD. If a video is to be shown at an event, it is imperative that the contract contain a definition for public performance rights. However, contractual language for public performance rights is not standardized, so it is important that this language be carefully reviewed to make sure that it meets the institution's needs. Finally, archival rights should be included in contracts for which perpetual access to a streaming video is purchased. Although there is currently no good solution to preserving digital video such as Portico or the HathiTrust, it is hoped that options will become available in the near future (farrelly 2016). In the meantime, preserving a non-circulating archival copy of a digital file in its original format is recommended (Duncan and Peterson 2014).

Managing Challenges

Large collections of vendor-hosted streaming videos are increasingly common and, on average, account for a greater percentage of academic library budgets than individual streaming titles (farrelly and Hutchison 2014). However, despite the increasing availability of large collections, many streaming video titles are available only as one-off purchases. Managing and maintaining oversight over these remain a challenge. This issue is especially challenging for institutions with a large number of individual titles that have been licensed over time, and it becomes even more complicated when these titles are not primarily licensed through one large vendor, such as Alexander Street Press or Kanopy. Because different films may be licensed for different length terms that will expire at various times during the year, digital streaming licenses expire regularly. Managing these expiration dates in the University of North Texas Media Library is a carefully orchestrated system that involves ILS reminders that automatically generate e-mail reminders, combined with a comprehensive spreadsheet containing all of the one-off videos that have been licensed since 2006. Each time a new digital streaming license is purchased, a license record is created in the ILS that tracks expiration dates and e-mails a reminder three months before each license is about to expire. This rigorous record-keeping system allows library staff to remain highly aware of streaming video license expirations, thereby minimizing issues with license renewals.

Negotiate to Meet Your Needs

Streaming video licensing, like all electronic resource licensing, is an intricate process that requires considerable knowledge of local contracting requirements and institutional needs, paired with a clear and efficient workflow, in order to be done well. This might seem like a daunting prospect at first, but most concerns about the streaming video licensing process can be overcome with a bit of practice and experience. One final point to keep in mind when dealing with streaming video license agreements is that the language of license agreements is always negotiable. If an institution has particular needs that are not being met by the standard language of a streaming video license agreement, it does no harm to ask the vendor for changes. Such requests are both important and necessary in order for libraries to achieve their ultimate goal of finding ways to best serve the needs of their users.

References

Duncan, Cheryl J., and Erika Day Peterson. 2014. *Creating a Streaming Video Collection for Your Library*. Lanham, MD: Rowman & Littlefield.

farrelly, deg. 2016. "Issues in Academic Library Streaming Video." *Journal of Digital Media Management* 5 (2): 169–81.

farrelly, deg, and Jane Hutchison. 2014. "Academic Library Streaming Video: Key Findings from the National Survey." *Against the Grain* 26 (5): 73–75.

King, Rachel. 2014. "House of Cards: The Academic Library Media Center in the Era of Streaming Video." *The Serials Librarian* 67 (3): 289–306.

Laskowski, Mary S. 2011. *Guide to Video Acquisitions in Libraries: Issues and Best Practices*. Chicago: ALCTS.

Leonard, Elizabeth. 2015. *Great Expectations: Students and Video in Higher Education*. Sage.

6

STREAMING VIDEO DISCOVERY IN ACADEMIC LIBRARIES

Scott Breivold

Today, with the advent and increased availability of high-speed Internet and the conversion of media to digital formats, brick-and-mortar music and video stores have all but disappeared. In the library world, obsolete media formats like VHS and Laserdisc are being weeded or eliminated entirely, and physical media are increasingly being housed and circulated at a centralized circulation/service desk. Just as print periodical acquisitions have given way to electronic journal/database subscriptions, we're beginning to see a marked shift away from physical media to acquiring online media content. Consequently, many media service points in libraries are disappearing or being repurposed as media production and/or maker spaces. Without media service points or visible browsing collections of physical media for patrons to peruse, how do libraries market and facilitate the discovery of their streaming video content? This chapter will focus on some of the challenges faced by academic libraries, although many of these considerations may be useful to public libraries as well.

THE CATALOG

Any exploration of "discovery" in the library context inevitably begins with the library catalog. Deg farrelly, a media librarian and streaming video expert at Arizona State University, zeroes in on this important aspect of streaming media content discovery when he writes, "It is essential to establish tools to identify and access this content without requiring users to search multiple access points or interfaces." In farrelly's view, "this is best accomplished through full MARC records in the library's catalog with direct links to the streaming file" (2014, 228). In a seminal Streaming Video Survey of 260 academic libraries conducted by farrelly and Surdi, 58.6 percent of the respondents indicated that they catalog streaming videos, and an additional 23.7 percent said they catalog "some" but not all streaming video content. When asked if they utilized title-level catalog records for streaming videos, 56.6 percent said yes if the title was licensed in perpetuity; 46.1 percent did so even with term-licensed titles; 63.8 percent cataloged titles in subscription collections; and 30.3 percent used catalog records for titles in collections purchased using patron/demand/evidence-driven acquisition models. The survey also asked about the primary source of streaming video catalog records. Of the libraries that cataloged streaming video titles, the largest number (65.1 percent) used vendor-provided MARC records, and 14.5 percent performed copy-cataloging using OCLC catalog records (farrelly and Surdi 2016). And as pointed out by CARLI committee members who wrote a white paper on streaming video in academic libraries, the issues that libraries should consider when adding catalog records for streaming video titles include the availability of vendor-supplied MARC records (as well as whether they are free or have a cost per title associated with each record—which can add up quickly with large collections); whether the video(s) have been purchased in perpetuity or licensed for a given period of time; and database maintenance concerns (such as associated costs; personnel, expertise, and workflow consid-erations related to modifying individual catalog records; adding or deleting titles from large streaming collections as vendor access/rights change, etc.) (Bossenga et al. 2013).

But even the concept of a library catalog search is rapidly evolving, as Henrietta Thornton-Verma pointed out: "Patrons are used to Google. They don't want to use different search methods to explore different databases. They don't even want to use different databases. Discovery services promise to enable all of a library's material, print and eBooks, journal articles, streaming video, everything, to be uncovered through one search box. It's different from the much-maligned federated search because instead of crawling through the catalog, then the databases . . . and so on, it compiles an enormous index of all of those things and searches it all at once" (Thornton-Verma 2011).

The 23-campus California State University system, for example, is in the process of rolling out a new unified library management system in which a "discovery layer" will be at the core of the user's information retrieval experience. The discovery layer approach builds a bridge between the more traditional online public access catalog (OPAC) and web-based search tools, enabling users to use a more simplified "one-stop shopping" interface to search vast collections of resources in all formats. Discovery tools allow the user to focus first on the search strategy, and second on the discovery of content and the refinement of search results. The use of facets in a discovery layer results page allows the searcher to easily narrow results by material type/format, subject, date, and so on. Behind the scenes, the discovery layer gathers data from a variety of metadata sources, including traditional MARC catalog records as well as indexed subscription database content and more. Web-scale discovery services (such as Primo, Summon, or EBSCO Discovery) can be costly for smaller institutions, but open-source options are beginning to emerge as well. Moving to the discovery layer platform may help resolve some of the cataloging concerns mentioned earlier, in that streaming video content may be indexed by the discovery platform's central knowledge base and may thus be discoverable without the need to upload full MARC records for each title (Bossenga et al. 2013). Deg farrelly points out, however, that "some larger distributors already work with discovery tool vendors to assure that their content is included. Libraries also need to work with discovery tool vendors to impress on them the importance of making video content discoverable and to ensure that their own collections are activated with the tools" (farrelly 2014, 228). In addition, farrelly makes the excellent observation that "link resolvers and authentication tools widely used to access journal papers and books identified by indexing databases could be applied to streaming video resources as well. By not indexing video content, the essential indexers of scholarly content are rendering video invisible to the academic researcher" (farrelly 2016, 6).

Librarians responsible for streaming video acquisitions are encouraged to work closely with cataloging or technical services experts to determine what level of quality, detail, and customization of catalog records works best for the institution and its users. Chapter 6 of Duncan and Peterson's book *Creating a Streaming Video Collection for Your Library* (2014) provides a good introduction to the various types of metadata used for library catalogs and discovery tools.

Another good resource for catalogers is the document "Best Practices for Cataloging Streaming Media Using RDA and MARC21" (Ho et al. 2015).

These days, the library catalog and/or discovery layer search box are usually front and center on an academic library's website. What surrounds that search box on the library's home page also shapes and directs the discovery experience for students and faculty who increasingly rely on 24/7 access to the library's resources via its website. With each new iteration of the library's web presence, it is important to invoke a number of design strategies to maximize efficiency (and discovery) for the user. Cal State LA (California State University, Los Angeles) has found it very useful to create library web design prototypes and to then conduct usability studies and focus groups with a broad section of users (including students from a variety of disciplines as well as faculty and staff). When considering the discovery of specific resources (like streaming video), a useful exercise would include usability/focus-group questions that focus on the format, so that data can be collected regarding a patron's ease or difficulty in locating such resources via the website's design structure. Library web designers are also benefiting from tools like Google Analytics to track visitors' behavior, and pinpoint the motivations behind their information-seeking (Fang 2007). Many streaming media vendors (like Kanopy, for example) provide excellent analytics tools, and library catalog or discovery layer vendors may include them as well. An examination of analytics data allows librarians to engage in "internal discovery" regarding their users' search behaviors, the popularity of particular resources, and so on. This information may be invaluable not only to guide purchase decisions, interface design, and library instruction, but also to identify potential marketing opportunities for a given resource, format, or platform.

Springshare's popular LibGuides product has become a staple in many academic libraries and also provides another useful tool for promoting streaming media resources broadly, as well as integrating them into subject- or course-specific research guides so that online video content can be accessed at the point of need. In the Streaming Video Survey of academic libraries, 71.9 percent reported that users located or accessed streaming videos via library LibGuides or Subject Guides (farrelly and Surdi 2016). A nice example of a LibGuide that provides an overview of all of a library's streaming video content is the guide created by Dan Stanton at Arizona State University: http://libguides.asu.edu/StreamingVideo. Users are provided with a definition of streaming video; information about accessing the content from off campus; detailed information about each of the major vendor platforms available and the content or subjects covered in each one; as well as a nice set of links to openly accessible Internet sites that provide academic streaming video content. In addition to the more comprehensive streaming video guides, subject-specific guides that provide information about or links to streaming content are another excellent way to assist students and faculty in locating the applicable video content for their discipline. The Prince George's Community College subject guide for nursing (http://pgcc.libguides.com/pgccnursing) contains a "Streaming Videos" tab that includes a link to their Medcom Video Training collection, as well as embedded search "widgets" that allow the user to search specific sections of the "Health & Medicine" subject category of "Films on Demand."

PROMOTING USE

Many academic libraries employ the subject specialist or "liaison" model to ensure that each department, program, or school has a librarian available to provide customized instruction for the discipline and work with faculty to select materials appropriate for their curricular and research needs. The library's subject specialists should become familiar with all of the streaming video content available so they can incorporate these resources into subject and course research guides, as well as highlight them in library instruction sessions. In writing about one library's "embedded librarian" approach, the authors observed, "The liaisons are the library's most successful marketing tool. Ongoing contact with the faculty gives them the opportunity both to learn about needs and gaps in service and to spread the word about the library's capabilities" (Freiburger and Kramer 2009, 141). Routinely, liaison librarians stay in close contact with their teaching faculty by attending departmental meetings, communicating via e-mail to announce new services and resources or to solicit suggestions and feedback regarding library acquisitions, serving on campus committees with them, and so on. The more that library subject specialists can don their marketing/public relations hat when working with faculty, the more likely they will begin to think about streaming videos and how they can incorporate them into their teaching (both in the classroom and via learning management systems such as Canvas or Moodle). The Streaming Video Survey of academic libraries reported that 64.1 percent of respondents utilized links to streaming videos in their online courses. In addition, 25.5 percent of institutions surveyed included links to streaming video content in their course reserves system (farrelly and Surdi 2016). Subject librarians should consider working directly with professors or via the campus faculty teaching and learning center to help identify and promote streaming media content that could be integrated into the campus learning management system so these resources are more visible to students at the point of need in their online courses.

As with most new library services or resources, promoting streaming videos and achieving optimal discovery by patrons requires a multipronged approach. In addition to the catalog or discovery layer and bibliographic record issues, academic libraries will also need to be creative when marketing their streaming video resources whether it be via the library website, social media, subject guides, learning management systems, displays, workshops, library instruction, or, of course, good old-fashioned word of mouth. In time, physical media formats will likely become secondary to online streaming media, but as we have seen with e-books, this will take time, and not all content will be digitized for many years to come. In the meantime, librarians will need to try and make informed decisions about which streaming video resources are the best fit for their institution, and what type and level of cataloging and record maintenance are appropriate given budgetary and personnel considerations. Librarians also need to continue to be advocates with vendors and patrons alike to ensure the maximum discoverability and use of streaming video content in order to maximize the cost-benefit ratio for these often costly subscription packages.

References

Bossenga, Susie, Chris Bulock, Luann Degreve, Carol Doyle, Tom Goetz, Ruth Lindemann, Stephen McMinn, and Charles Uth. 2013. "Streaming Video in Academic Libraries: A White Paper." CARLI Commercial Products Committee. https://www.carli.illinois.edu/sites/files/files/2014CommercialProductsCommStreamingVideoinAcademicLibraries.pdf.

Duncan, Cheryl J., and Erika Day Peterson. 2014. *Creating a Streaming Video Collection for Your Library*. Lanham, MD: Rowman & Littlefield.

Fang, Wei. 2007. "Using Google Analytics for Improving Library Website Content and Design: A Case Study." *Library Philosophy and Practice* 121. http://digitalcommons.unl.edu/libphilprac/121.

farrelly, deg. 2014. "Streaming Video." In *Rethinking Collection Development and Management*, edited by Becky Albitz, Christine Avery, and Diane Zabel, 215–32. Santa Barbara, CA: Libraries Unlimited.

———. 2016. "Issues in Academic Library Streaming Video." *Journal of Digital Media Management* 5 (2): 1–13.

farrelly, deg, and Jane Hutchinson Surdi. 2016. "Academic Library Streaming Video Revisited." Arizona State University Libraries. https://repository.asu.edu/items/39058.

Freiburger, Gary, and Sandra Kramer. 2009. "Embedded Librarians: One Library's Model for Decentralized Service." *Journal of the Medical Library Association* 97 (2): 139–42.

Ho, Jeannette, Erminia Chao, Rebecca Culbertson, Jennifer Eustis, Cyrus Ford Zarganji, Annie Glerum, Ngoc-My Guidarelli, Mary Huismann, Stacie Traill, and Donna Viscuglia. 2015. "Best Practices for Cataloging Streaming Media Using RDA and MARC21," 1–125. Online Audiovisual Catalogers Inc. (OLAC), Cataloging Policy Committee (CAPC). http://digitalscholarship.unlv.edu/lib_articles/483.

Thornton-Verma, H. 2011. "Discovering What Works: Librarians Compare Discovery Interface Experiences." *Library Journal.* http://reviews.libraryjournal.com/2011/12/reference/discovering-what-works-librarians-compare-discovery-interface-experiences.

USAGE ANALYSIS AND ASSESSMENT OF STREAMING VIDEO

Mary Gilbertson and Tim Jiping Zou

The digital age has pushed usage analysis increasingly to the forefront in the assessment of collections. Just as journals and books are progressively more electronic, so too is video. While the thought of user analysis usually brings to mind charts and graphs of statistics about the resources purchased by the library, user analysis should begin with understanding users' needs. What is the experience of the representative user? What is the curriculum that needs to be supported? Does the platform support the way users search and work? The type of library, research interests, and current trends all affect the use of materials.

BACKGROUND OF VIDEO ASSESSMENT

The assessment of the use of physical media collections, which generally refers to DVDs for the purposes of this study, traditionally relies on circulation statistics generated from the ILS system. Few studies have been dedicated to assessing the use of a library's DVD collection, other than general reports of the trends in circulation of DVDs and VHS titles, and there is an obvious lack of a benchmark type of study across all sectors of the library. In public libraries, DVDs generate a larger number of circulations than in academic libraries, since the purpose of the collections in the two types of libraries are totally different—one for recreation, and the other for instruction and research. At the Kansas Public Library, for example, DVDs accounted for almost 60 percent of the circulation, although the DVD collection constitutes only 7.6 percent of total adult holdings of the library (Annoyed Librarian 2010). Due to the ephemeral nature of the usage of videos, it is not necessarily wise to reject the purchase of a streaming video because the library already owns the title in the DVD format, but it is also not critical to replace a title already owned as a DVD with a streaming video in an academic setting. A title that is already owned on DVD could be needed for online courses and remote access. Additionally, there is no return on investment (ROI) justification to select "interesting" titles in case they might be of interest to faculty and students.

While individual libraries count the usage of DVDs locally, some standard surveys such as the Library Journal Budget Survey (https://s3.amazonaws.com/WebVault/research/2016_LJ_Budget_Survey.pdf) have tended to include DVD circulation data in the total generic circulation for the reporting period. Some public libraries purposefully consider boosting circulation statistics by acquiring many popular motion-picture DVDs and lending them for short loan periods.

PURPOSE OF A VIDEO COLLECTION IN ACADEMIC LIBRARIES

In the academic library world, the traditional method of usage assessment continues, but it has been challenged. The value of the library's collection and services is generally measured by the titles held; that is, those cataloged, managed, and maintained by the library. But more and more libraries share collections through the HathiTrust, for example, or through consortia, and they participate in patron-driven acquisitions (PDA) models, in which titles are purchased only after the usage meets a set threshold, all of which further blurs the distinction of assessment. PDA is a popular purchase method because this technique provides a large pool of titles for users to choose from, and it takes some of the guesswork out of selection. This premise seems especially helpful in providing increased access to streaming videos of popular titles. Libraries may choose to load records for the HathiTrust or from PDA programs. However, the Association of Research Libraries' (ARL's) 2015–2016 annual statistical report survey specifically instructs librarians to not report usage statistics for titles for which the library is not providing sustained stewardship and maintenance.

WHAT TO MEASURE:
FROM CIRCULATION COUNT TO ROI

Two of the efforts for the assessment of library acquisitions and services seem to be the most-discussed concepts: *return on investment (ROI)*, which addresses maximizing limited materials budgets to serve the various needs of library users; and the *user experience*, which strives to provide competitive, effective content discovery and delivery services utilizing the available technology.

The need to assess and measure the value of a library's resources and the users' experience certainly has evolved along with the emergence of digital libraries. In the last decade, the size of the DVD/VHS collection, and the circulation and course reserve totals, have been the essential data for annual reports to the governing institution as well as professional associations for determining (1) how library resources are being used, (2) the need for budget appropriation or adjustment, and (3) the overall assessment of the value of the investment. DVD video collection usage statistics are not separately reported and analyzed in the reporting structures that are typically used for academic libraries, such as ARL and Association of College & Research Libraries (ACRL) statistics. They are just part of the total gross print monograph circulation counts in terms of total volumes.

As with streaming videos by and large, the hard-copy DVD collection in academic libraries has been defined as a *working collection* to address the specific curriculum needs of the institution. A comprehensive collection of films in all genres and documentaries is neither necessary nor fiscally practical because traditionally, academic librarians have tended to exclude popular videos which, although proven to be a major boost to the circulation count in public libraries, are still broadly considered to be unsuitable for the academic library. "Assessing how popular culture items contribute to the educational mission of an academic institution is difficult to measure by traditional library assessment tools that assume easily measured inputs and outputs" (Dimmock 2007, 144).

Among academic libraries, core title lists are also not available for videos and other media resources. One can conclude that this is among the reasons why the ACRL does not suggest any quantitative measurement of a media collection in the current "Guidelines for Media Resources in Academic Libraries" (Laskowski et al. 2012). The "Guidelines" stress that a media resource collection policy should address the specific needs of academic programs and services; it should define qualitative criteria instead of quantitative criteria; and "it should incorporate benchmarks by which a particular library and information service, resource, or material may be judged" (Laskowski et al. 2012). Albitz maintains that "media centers are established as working collections, not as archives. If these collections go unused, then the mission of the institution goes unsupported" (2001, 6). Even so, academic libraries have tended to define their multimedia collections as archives and therefore have inhibited user access. Many libraries have kept media materials in closed shelving with a limited circulation policy (Brancolini and Provine 1993). One of the reasons for this was that multimedia materials require playback devices and are subject to damage when used outside of the library (Intner and Smiraglia 1994).

It can likewise be reasoned that the size of a streaming media collection should not be used as a key assessment factor, since there are no recommended core publications for acquisitions among academic libraries. When academic libraries struggled with determining the relative efficacy of e-journal databases and other electronic resource packages, librarians took into consideration the impact factor (a measure of the frequency of citations an average article receives in a journal over a particular period). Using this consideration, a lesser-used journal title can still be retained if it has a high impact factor and the number of journals published in the subject field is small. However, this approach is not applicable for selecting or de-selecting books and e-book packages because whether a title is considered a core or major publication in the field is subject to the book reviewer's or the subject librarian's review (Grigg 2012). The impact factor is also likely irrelevant when selecting and de-selecting titles in streaming video models. An additional challenge with the streaming video marketing models is licensing to play instead of licensing to own. The nature of licensing to play causes the purchase of media to be demand-driven.

ECONOMIC MODELS AND COST PER USE

When libraries start to implement streaming video services, the most frequently asked questions are related to the costs. The various and unpredictable terms of use in streaming licenses, the price for subscribing to packaged videos and services, the PDA model which often leads to an open-ended budget and expenditure, not to mention the staffing time and technical support, are all issues that contribute to the cost. This leads to the critical concern of many: is the streaming video service a viable and sustainable program for our library? Can we afford it? The answers to these questions vary according to a library's mission, priority, and budget. While academic libraries tend not to assess the ROI for the hard-copy DVD collection, it becomes imperative to understand ROI when libraries contemplate the implementation of a streaming media service, because their administrators use this measure in decision-making. An analysis of the ROI of the DVD collection at Simmons College and the University of Massachusetts at Amherst reveals a surprisingly low usage of the DVD collection as measured by lifetime checkouts. The study also finds an identical pattern at both libraries that the DVD collection loses relevance over time (Erdmann, Ferguson, and Stangroom 2015). The study's analysis used a formula to assess the ROI of their DVD collection:

DVD average cost + shipping processing costs / number of circulation
= ROI

A comparison of ROI between streaming video and DVD shows that the PDA streaming video purchase model is much more cost-effective than the purchase "just-in-case" DVD acquisition model (see figure 7.1). "Purchased Collection," in this figure, refers to a situation in which an entire package of streaming films is bought in perpetuity for a fixed price, and this is also not as cost-effective as the PDA model in this case. (Keep in mind that this study is based on academic pricing with performance rights.) Streaming video purchased on demand ensures maximum and unlimited use and reduces the per-play cost, as demonstrated by figure 7.1, which demonstrates plays per paid film (ROI) from the Erdmann, Ferguson, and Stangroom study.

Another study conducted at the University of Arkansas in 2014 analyzes the ROI by examining cost per use (CPU) between the DVD collection, subscription models of streaming video, and a PDA model of streaming media (Zou and Gilbertson 2015). This study did not include shipping and processing costs to establish an average CPU based on the total usage of all titles in the DVD collection, and it arrived at a CPU of $6.44 for that collection. The CPU for streaming media cost was then compared. The result of the study suggests that on average, the streaming media CPU was lower than that of the average DVD. For the PDA model, the CPU ranged from $1.08 to $37.50 per license

		UMass	Simmons
Kanopy PDA	Plays per Triggered Film	109	105
	ROI ($/play)[1]	$1.38	$1.28
DVD	Lifetime Checkouts / DVD	7.2	5.9
	ROI ($/checkout)[2]	$18.15	$20.15
Purchased Collection	Plays per film	0.01	0.10
	(ROI ($/play)[3]	$264.20	–

[1] A play is defined as 30 seconds or more viewed
[2] Checkout is a checkout from the library irrespective if played
[3] Upfront payment with ongoing annual fees. Plays per film per year since available (declining year on year)

Figure 7.1 | **Plays per paid film (ROI)**

triggered, with an average per-use cost of $5.46. The more the triggered title is used, the lower the CPU. For a subscription collection, it is important that the library subscribe to a package that is sure to be used. More titles in the collection usually mean more up-front cost. While overall streaming costs are not inexpensive, the per-view costs have been reasonable at the University of Arkansas, as shown in figure 7.2.

Whether a library has implemented or plans to implement a streaming video service, it is important to recognize that such a service is primarily demand-driven and the collection is a working collection. There are several important reasons to support this philosophy. The cost of providing a streaming video service is mainly for acquiring streaming licenses, regardless of the various terms of use negotiated with content providers. Even though a library may be able to purchase the licenses of certain titles with perpetual access rights, the majority of the digital media content is offered to libraries with a limited term of access. The library does not own the digital content. Once the licensed term expires, access to the content is discontinued. This is one reason why a streaming video service should not be considered as a replacement for an existing DVD collection.

Furthermore, titles that are requested and used many times during one year don't necessarily guarantee repeated use in the future, supporting the premise that videos that don't meet specific and sometimes temporal curricular needs

Streaming Source	# of Titles	# of plays	CPU
Subscription #1	2580	726	$1.60
PDA - Kanopy	13,219	1098	$5.46
Subscription #2	14,938	3074	$6.08

Figure 7.2 | **University of Arkansas streaming cost per use**

should not be "collected." This policy suggestion was discussed by Handman (2010) in "License to Look: Evolving Models for Library Video Acquisitions and Access." The author briefly defines three types of collection models: (1) just-in-case, (2) just-in-time, and (3) general circulating. Defining the video-on-demand model of acquisition, Handman emphasizes that the "transition from ownership of collections of physical media to a service-based model of access of licensed resources will require rethinking the budgeting process." Assessing return on investment is a critical step in measuring the cost-effectiveness of the streaming video service and collection while rethinking the budgeting process.

ROI AND TYPES OF LICENSES

The various types of licenses available for streaming video complicate usage analysis and assessing the return on investment for this format. The earlier implementers of streaming media services usually started with small, locally hosted collections that were developed in-house. By contrast, managing licenses with various distributors is more challenging. The types of license terms differ by vendors, and models of service vary accordingly and require a significant amount of time to review. Usually, the single-title type of licensing method is expensive. Schroeder and Williamsen (2011) found in their study that the price ranged from "$200 to $700 per title, averaging out to $407 per license." Additionally, distributors often change license fees as new marketing strategies are developed.

As the streaming media market matures, aggregator video packages have emerged to offer comprehensive collections and subject-specific sub-collections. The advantage of aggregator packages is that they more easily allow a library to integrate the video content with a library discovery platform; by contrast, title-by-title licenses are served through Blackboard or some other local hosting platform and are not available for the general public to discover. Negotiating with distributors on a title-by-title basis could result in longer turnaround time, whereas negotiating a packaged subscription or a PDA service could ensure consistency in license price and an overall use license. Conversely, as the streaming media market gains momentum, service providers have already revised their marketing strategies. Librarians will need to adapt their assessment to incorporate these changes for cross-comparisons.

ROI AND INTANGIBLE VALUES

The assessment of ROI should also take into consideration the intangible but intended values that the services entail by finding answers to such questions as:

- Does the service address the user expectations and demand for 24/7 access?
- Does the selected collection(s) fit the curriculum needs and equally support online and on-campus courses?
- Does the model(s) of service provide MARC records that enable the integration of indexing into the library discovery system and that enable easy and seamless search and discovery?
- Does the service support access through mobile devices?
- Does the collection have a closed-caption option for accessibility?
- Does the service provide usage reports and analysis tools?
- Does the service support seamless proxy authentication for user access off campus?
- Does the service offer online tutorials?

These questions are all directly related to the intended technology-enabled values. Because these values are intangible, many libraries measure them by conducting user surveys to gain an overall understanding of the ROI.

User surveys should not be underestimated and should be employed periodically to obtain qualitative measurement of direct responses to specific questions about how students and faculty have met their learning and instructional needs, as well as their experience of using the service. Unsolicited feedback should also not be excluded, since it could be invaluable.

METHODS OF ASSESSMENT AND METRICS

Until recently, there had not been a standard and commonly agreed-upon method of assessment for streaming media. Browsing or clicking the title to read information about a video does not mean the user actually watched the video, although one can draw an analogy to the same situation with circulating DVDs in that there is no way to determine if a circulated video is actually watched. Comparatively, deep log data for accessing digital media allows separate reports of searches from views. It is important to determine what data element to use for reporting and assessment.

It is even more difficult to compare the usage data of multiple sources or platforms. One principal challenge of user analysis is establishing a quantitative model to compare across platforms. The definitions of "search" and "session" from streaming usage reports may vary from platform to platform. "While title level usage data provided by vendors indicates what is popular, there are no ways to connect titles to specific users and their demographics, including which class was assigned to watch a film. Further investigations into who is using streaming video would be particularly insightful. Current statistics from Kanopy, for example, confirm that most usage is class-driven, the most watched films are diverse, interdisciplinary, and provide little guidance for future collection development or answering the question of who uses the films" (Morris and Currie 2016).

In response to this difficulty, the COUNTER (Counting Online Usage of NeTworked Electronic Resources) Code of Practice (https://www.project-counter.org/about/) has been established to enable publishers and vendors to report the usage of their electronic resources in a consistent manner. It allows librarians to compare data received from different COUNTER-compliant publishers and vendors. It also helps librarians use this data to demonstrate the value of electronic resources. COUNTER usage reports pertaining to multimedia usage statistics are found in section 4, 4.1.4., release 4 of the Code of Practice. It employs two methods of calculating usage statistics.

1. Multimedia Report 1 (MR1) counts the number of successful full multimedia content unit requests by month and collection (see figure 7.3).
2. Multimedia Report 2 (MR2) counts the number of successful full multimedia content unit requests by month, collection, and item type (see figure 7.4).

Multimedia Report 1 (R4)			Number of Successful Multimedia Full Content Unit Requests by Month and Collection			
<Customer>						
<Institutional Identifier>						
Period covered by Report:						
yyyy-mm-dd to yyyy-mm-dd						
Date run:						
yyyy-mm-dd						
Collection	Content Provider	Platform	Reporting Period Total	Jan-2011	Feb-2011	Mar-2011
Total for all Collections			4282	264	536	256
Collection AA	Provider X	Platform Z	2452	174	266	187
Collection BB	Provider X	Platform Z	708	56	102	30
Collection CC	Provider Y	Platform Z	200	10	31	7
Collection DD	Provider Y	Platform Z	922	24	137	32

Figure 7.3 | **Multimedia Report 1 (MR1) example**

If multimedia content is provided through a consortial subscription, the usage data is presented in a single report, with data broken down by the consortium members.

Alexander Street Press was the first streaming vendor to provide COUNTER-compliant reports. Alexander Street now offers a new usage statistics portal to obtain usage information of collections on a new interface that includes COUNTER 4-compliant reports, SUSHI-enabled reports, and customized reports that can be exported by title, subject, and collection. More information about Alexander Street usage statistics can be found at https://alexanderstreet.com/page/usage-statistics. SUSHI stands for Standardized Usage Statistics Harvesting Initiative. SUSHI allows for the automated retrieval of the COUNTER usage reports into local systems, which should make the harvesting and aggregating of usage reports much less time-consuming.

In addition to a report on the total and monthly counts of playbacks, Alexander Street Press provides customized reports on playbacks by (1) subject area, (2) collection (and sub-collections), (3) title playbacks by subject area, and (4) title playbacks by collection. (See figure 7.5.) COUNTER-compliant providers report the count either by playbacks, or by separating the number of searches from the actual number of playbacks. When reporting or comparing usage data across different products, one must be sure to use playback as the counting unit in order to avoid skewing the usage statistics by including searches and browsing.

Multimedia Report 2 (R4)	Number of Successful Full Multimedia Content Unit Requests by Month, Collection and Item Type						
<Customer>							
<Institutional Identifier>							
Period covered by Report:							
yyyy-mm-dd to yyyy-mm-dd							
Date run:							
yyyy-mm-dd							
Collection	Content Provider	Platform	Item Type	Reporting Period Total	Jan-2011	Feb-2011	Mar-2011
Total for all Collections	Provider X	Platform Z	Non-textual resource: audio	2594	386	235	80
Total for all Collections	Provider X	Platform Z	Non-textual resource: image	770	15	618	5
Total for all Collections	Provider X	Platform Z	Non-textual resource: video	21344	2487	1606	678
Total for all Collections	Provider X	Platform Z	Non-textual resource: other	221	50	8	0
Collection AA	Provider X	Platform Z	Non-textual resource: audio	17149	174	266	187
Collection AA	Provider X	Platform Z	Non-textual resource: image	708	56	102	30
Collection AA	Provider X	Platform Z	Non-textual resource: video	200	10	31	7
Collection AA	Provider X	Platform Z	Non-textual resource: other	922	24	137	32
Collection BB	Provider X	Platform Z	Non-textual resource: audio	2452	2246	580	452
Collection BB	Provider X	Platform Z	Non-textual resource: image	51	28	5	2
Collection BB	Provider X	Platform Z	Non-textual resource: video	950	148	80	28
Collection BB	Provider X	Platform Z	Non-textual resource: other	327	64	7	14

Figure 7.4 | **Multimedia Report 2 (MR2) example**

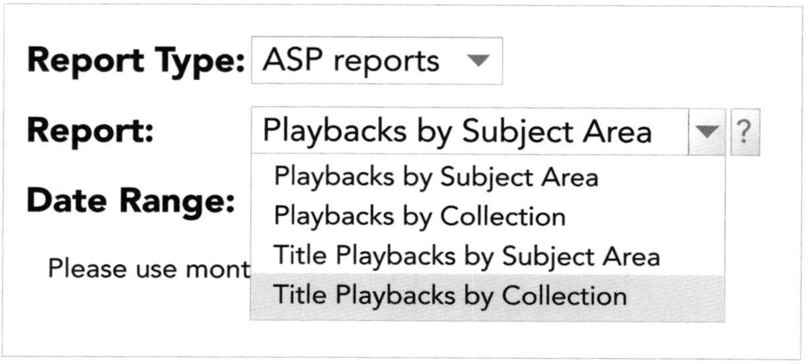

Figure 7.5 | **COUNTER reports—playback**

OVERLAP ANALYSIS

Overlap analysis is an important aspect of assessment for the demand-driven e-book environment, since the purpose of patron-driven acquisition is to pay for titles that are actually used. However, purchasing multiple copies and duplications through the PDA method is in conflict with the idea of cost-effective acquisitions. E-book distributors usually build into their products overlap analysis tools that provide librarians with information about unique holdings and duplications. In the streaming video service environment, overlap is unavoidable in the sense that libraries often purchase multiple formats: DVD and access through licensing for performance or streaming rights of the same content. This dilemma is unique for the multimedia market. With streaming media products and services, large aggregators such as the Naxos Music Library and the Classical Music Library by Alexander Street Press have digitized a large number of videos that are already owned in other formats. One should conclude that overlap analysis would also be built into streaming PDA services. However, streaming video vendors do not readily offer to perform overlap analysis across delivery platforms. Nevertheless, de-duplication efforts should be made where possible.

USER ENGAGEMENT

Usage analysis alone should not determine the ROI and the impact on institutional learning and instruction. In a digital library environment, a new layer of assessment commonly known as "user engagement" has been widely discussed. User engagement assessment attempts to evaluate library users' experiences when interacting with resources, as well as with content discovery and the delivery interface. The measurement of how the service meets users' expectations should also be part of the metrics.

User engagement assessment requires librarians to look beyond the usage count to include other system log data that reveals how users interact with content. Useful data elements together with user surveys help librarians gain an understanding of when and how users use the streamed content and service. Kanopy Streaming Service, for example, has versatile analytic tools to allow librarians to easily generate system log data in three categories:

USAGE	AUDIENCE	ENGAGEMENT
• Summary	• Countries	• Summary
• Daily Activity	• Browsers	• Comments
• Videos	• Devices	• Ratings
• Subjects	• On-Off Campus	• Playlists
• Suppliers	• Days of the Week	• Watch Lists
• PDA Performance	• Hours of the Day	
	• Referral URLs	
	• Search Keywords	

The assessment of streaming video becomes feasible and manageable with these reporting tools. The summary report presents an overall view of how users interact with the content during a librarian-defined time period; the other report headings allow librarians to drill in to specific statistical sets in order to get some snapshots. Kanopy allows librarians to compare two data elements—film title pages viewed, and film title played—to gauge the level of user engagement. Because of its reporting tools, several studies on the PDA model have become available. While other providers have been improving their usage reporting tools following Kanopy's lead, librarians can always ask for raw data to create reports along the three categories if needed.

BENCHMARKING

One method used for assessment in ARL libraries is benchmarking to compare the quality of a library's collections against those of other libraries. Benchmarking assessment is usually meaningful when the comparison is made between libraries identified as peer institutions. Knowing the performance of our libraries compared to others assists us in meeting objectives and sharing ideas. When selecting peer institutions for benchmarking the collection, Karen Grigg (2012) suggests looking into their comparability in four factors:

- Size of the library
- Similarity of the subject areas covered
- Size of the budget allocation
- Ranking of the libraries

Benchmarking may not be as meaningful for a streaming video collection as it is for a physical (DVD) collection, since the purpose of streaming media is to provide access, while that of a DVD collection is to gain ownership of copies. Moreover, large academic libraries have a different mix of streaming media resources, which could present challenges for benchmarking analysis when comparing oranges with apples. However, the literature review has yielded a few benchmark studies on the PDA model. The Cleary, Humphrey, and Bates (2014) study began in 2013 to compare the PDA acquisition trials at the Queensland University of Technology and La Trobe University, focusing on the relevancy of content, discoverability, accessibility, and affordability. These studies provided input for Kanopy to refine the PDA content pricing model and service platform. In the United States, several studies were conducted around 2014 when Kanopy rolled out its U.S. service.

An assessment of the consortial PDA pilot program in the Western New York Library Resources Council was published in 2016. The assessment compares reflections on the pilot program written by three different parties involved in the program that aimed to provide a holistic perspective on its performance and outcomes (Knab, Humphrey, and Ward 2016). The collaborative effort to explore ways for a cost-effective streaming media service provides some insight into the challenges and further expectations of the pilot program. Although these were academic libraries supporting college undergraduate degrees, the participating libraries all had their own objectives and expectations. It was difficult to identify usage patterns both in terms of demand for specific content and the number of plays because the academic programs are not quite comparable, and this may have contributed to the difficulty of applying the benchmarking approach. Outcomes from comparing the on-demand usage at the eight participating libraries show that use of the streaming titles was driven by faculty selection for class reading and assignment, and perhaps because of this factor, the films triggered continued to be watched, which heightened the overall ROI. Since the PDA titles were selected, managed, and accessed from the same platform, the deep log data allows the comparison of users' searching and viewing behavior in terms of where and how, when, and how long users watched online. The study also provides an assessment of the consortial cost-sharing model. While the data did not prove a significant advantage in cost reduction, it presented an uneven distribution of fund contribution and usage. While five libraries showed that their users used less than their contribution to the deposit account, two libraries reported more usage than their contributions (see figure 7.6).

A larger-scaled benchmark analysis was also conducted among large ARL member libraries on the use of the Kanopy collection and service. The results of this study were presented at the 2016 ALA Annual Conference. For this benchmark study, the group aimed to use the Kanopy analytic tool to compare "one's analytics to those of other institutions or key standards" (Humphrey 2016). The same study intended to establish a benchmarking assessment that is applicable to peer groups, consortia, or direct peer-to-peer comparison. A more challenging aspect of the benchmark analytics is to define metrics. COUNTER has established standard metrics for e-journals (e.g., searches, sessions, downloads, download per session, search per session). The Kanopy benchmark study intends to better use the server transactional log and the analytics tools to gain a fuller understanding of users' impression of the collection and service. Several potential measurements can be benchmarked (see figure 7.7).

MEASURING COLLECTIONS

A circulation count of the physical video collection has been traditionally used as the key indicator of the value of such a collection. The circulation count also correlates to the gate count, since use of the physical collection requires users to visit the library. In a digital media library environment, the two important measurements have shifted to the count of online visits of the service (the visit and review) compared to the actual plays of the content. Even though libraries continue to add new acquisitions to their DVD collections, the shift to acquire

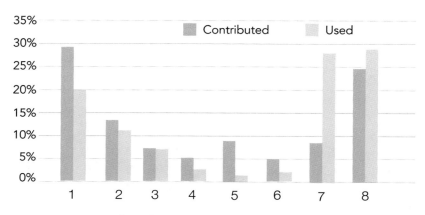

Figure 7.6 | **Contributed percentage and usage by library**

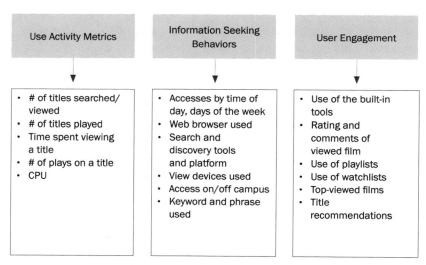

Figure 7.7 | **Potential measurements for benchmark analysis**

access (licensed to view) video has fundamentally changed the way we provide service. If users cannot find titles and do not use them, the collection is of no value to them. User studies are thus critical, and the user activity analytics are most useful for measuring whether the content addresses the needs of the users.

MEASURING SERVICE QUALITY AND USER EXPERIENCE

The data on users' information-seeking behavior provides quantitative measurements for librarians to analyze user behavior patterns and gain a better understanding of the following:

- Where do users start the search for streaming video content?
- How easily can the users learn to use the discovery platforms?
- How effectively and efficiently can the users use the discovery tools to locate what they want?
- What kind of viewing devices are used to play the film?
- What is their viewer behavior in terms of browsing, playing, creating a playlist, and commenting on or rating the films?

MEASURING THE IMPACT

Increasingly, the studies on streaming media service and acquisition models have shifted to streaming media's impact on learning and instruction as collection managers have adapted to data-driven acquisitions and budget allocation. A big challenge for assessing the library's impact lies in the defining performance indicators, whether they are quantitatively or qualitatively measurable (Mezick 2007). While librarians can cite the remarkable increase in the use of streaming videos and the strong demand from faculty for video content to be available in digital formats, media resources and budgets are only part of the library's overall services and expenditures. The success and impact of the media service, as subsets of either monographs (one-time resource purchases) or serials and databases (ongoing resource purchases), is often condensed to a usage count in the library's annual reports or its report to the professional organization (Lindauer 1998). Report elements for e-books have been added in ARL and ACRL reporting, but there is no separate assessment data to track the change and impact in streaming media. It is therefore up to the media and subject librarians' extra efforts to provide evidence specifically relevant to streaming video, and to document their findings in a meaningful way. In addition to ROI analysis, potential assessment factors could include, but are not limited to, the following aspects:

- Relevancy of the content to the instructional activities in terms of titles searched and viewed.
- Content traditionally used for DVD reserve versus content provided and used from a digital format.
- Impact of the online videos on online courses as well as on on-campus face-to-face instruction.
- Analysis of the trends of content used in relation to academic programs and disciplines.
- Trends in faculty demand for streaming video content across academic departments and disciplines.
- Patterns of searching and use of the online video content in relation to course syllabus and reading assignments.

Vendors are now moving beyond usage statistics and are developing ways to increase and measure users' engagement with video content. If videos are being used in the middle of the day, we may be able to conclude that they are being used for class-related purposes rather than for entertainment, since most people view videos for entertainment in the evening. Peaks in usage during the semester and lower activity during breaks also indicate that the videos are being used for class-related purposes. Viewing only sections of a film and pauses may also indicate that the film is being explored in relation to a class.

User surveys could yield valuable information for librarians to assess comparable products. The users' perception and experience of using the content and service, together with usage counts, as well as the licensing model and cost analysis, could all help librarians make data-driven budgetary decisions. Specific situations where such data could help include reallocating the budget from print collections to digital access, renegotiating subscriptions by dropping certain sub-collections, or choosing which subject areas to purchase. The end goal is to achieve cost-effective collections and service.

CONCLUSION

Electronic publishing has vastly affected all areas of collection development in all types of libraries. The streaming media service, together with the content the service provides, is a significant breakthrough in media content storage, distribution, and delivery technology that has accelerated the transition from hard-copy media to the online dissemination of media content. However, offering materials to academic library users that they don't need for their coursework could turn into a costly endeavor. Although providing access to large collections of streaming video is not always the less expensive option overall, it does meet the needs of the digital scholar and keeps in step with the evolution of the technological structure in which libraries deliver information in the research process. "When combined, digital media plus the Internet means that an audio or video file with intrinsic value could be sold and delivered directly to anyone in the world with an Internet connection—more potential customers than ever could fit into even the largest of retail stores" (Rayburn and Hoch 2005). Streaming video service in academic libraries has been developed based on the same promise. Unlike the shift from print books to that of e-books, streaming video content generally is not collectable. It has become a license-to-view type of service. If a contract for the service discontinues, so will the content. Therefore, the value of the service is not only defined by the size and depth of the collection, but also by the curricular relevancy of the content and the quality of the service.

Usage analysis related to media and streaming video is complicated. Libraries will likely continue to attempt to provide a complete representation of what content is used the most, with the expectation that limited budgets will be spent on those resources with the highest usage. It is the media manager's obligation to convey the differences in streaming media evaluation. A part of this is reporting the traditional assessment measurements such as usage, size of collection, relevancy, and quality, but it also requires conveying the message that streaming collections increase access to media materials that traditionally had access limits, and that the media collection is a working collection.

References

Albitz, Rebecca S. 2001. "Establishing Access Policies for Emerging Media in Academic Libraries." *Collection Management* 25 (3): 1–9. doi:10.1300/J105v25n03_01.

Annoyed Librarian. 2010. "Library Videos Won't Survive, and There Go Our Circ Stats." *Library Journal.* http://lj.libraryjournal.com/blogs/annoyedlibrarian/2010/09/22/videos-circ-stats/.

Brancolini, Kris, and Rick Provine. 1993. *Video Collections and Multimedia in ARL Libraries.* Washington, DC: Association of Research Libraries, Office of Management Services.

Cleary, Colleen, Olivia Humphrey, and Alison Bates. 2014. "Possible, Inevitable or Fait Accompli? An Analysis of Streaming Video Acquisition Acceptance and Use in Higher Education." In *VALA 2014 [Conference]*, edited by Alyson Kosina, 1–15. Melbourne, Australia. https://eprints.qut.edu.au/66331/123/66331.pdf.

Dimmock, Nora. 2007. "A Popular DVD Collection in an Academic Library." *New Library World* 108 (3/4): 141–50. doi:10.1108/03074800710735348.

Erdmann, Annie, Jennifer Ferguson, and Scott Stangroom. 2015. "Putting Your Patrons in the Driver's Seat: Assessing the Value of On-Demand Streaming Video." https://www.slideshare.net/jferguson7/putting-your-patrons-in-the-drivers-seat-with-online-video.

Grigg, Karen. 2012. "Assessment and Evaluation of E-Book Collections." In *Building and Managing E-Book Collections*, edited by Richard Kaplan, 127–37. Chicago: Neal-Schuman.

Handman, Gary. 2010. "License to Look: Evolving Models for Library Video Acquisition and Access." *Library Trends* 58 (3): 324–34.

Humphrey, Tom. 2016. "Impact Analytics and Benchmarking: A 14-Library Study into the Future of Resource Assessment." Panel discussion presented at the Annual Conference of the American Library Association, Orlando, FL.

Intner, Sheila S., and Richard P. Smiraglia. 1994. *Circulation Policy in Academic, Public, and School Libraries.* Westport, CT: Greenwood.

Knab, Sheryl, Tom Humphrey, and Caryl Ward. 2016. "Now Streaming: A Consortial PDA Video Pilot Project." *Collaborative Librarianship* 8 (1): 41–54. http://digitalcommons.du.edu/collaborativelibrarianship/vol8/iss1/8.

Laskowski, Mary S., Cyrus Ford, Nancy E. Friedland, Jacqueline Fritz, Jim Holmes, Lora Lennertz Jetton, M. Claire Stewart, and Joe M. Williams. 2012. "Guidelines for Media Resources in Academic Libraries." Association of College & Research Libraries. www.ala.org/acrl/standards/mediaresources.

Library Journal. 2016. "2016 Budget Survey." https://s3.amazonaws.com/WebVault/research/2016_LJ_Budget_Survey.pdf.

Lindauer, Bonnie G. 1998. "Defining and Measuring the Library's Impact and Campuswide Outcomes." *College & Research Libraries* 59 (6): 546–70. http://crl.acrl.org/index.php/crl/article/view/15249.

Mezick, Elizabeth M. 2007. "Return on Investment: Libraries and Student Retention." *The Journal of Academic Librarianship* 33 (5): 561–66.

Morris, Sara E., and Lea H. Currie. 2016. "To Stream or Not to Stream." *New Library World* 117 (7/8): 485–98.

Rayburn, Dan, and Michael Hoch. 2005. *The Business of Streaming and Digital Media.* Burlington, MA: Focal.

Schroeder, Rebecca, and Julie Williamsen. 2011. "Streaming Video: The Collaborative Convergence of Technical Services, Collection Development, and Information Technology in the Academic Library." *Collection Management* 36 (2): 89–106. doi:10.1080/01462679.2011.554128.

Zou, Tim, and Mary Gilbertson. 2015. "Demystifying the DDA Acquisition Model for Online Videos: In the University of Arkansas Case." Presentation at the National Media Market Annual Meeting, Albuquerque, New Mexico, October.

8

CLASSROOM USE

Mary Wahl

S treaming video is playing an increasingly large role in education. The format allows educators to assign viewings as homework as part of a flipped classroom method. Students appreciate the flexibility of 24/7 availability that streaming video offers, and libraries benefit from the ability to simultaneously serve multiple users on high-use titles. Streaming video is fast becoming an expected part of a library's collection if it serves any level of education.

Video in general enjoys a number of permissions as applied to the instructional use of copyrighted materials. However, the permissions become more complex once streaming and distance education enter the conversation. Libraries will no doubt receive questions regarding the use of streaming video in the traditional classroom and beyond. Thus, it is important for those working with the format to have an understanding of the basic principles of copyright and exemptions such as the TEACH Act and fair use.

COPYRIGHT

Copyright is a bundle of rights that provides content creators with exclusive rights over the use and distribution of their work for a limited time. In the United States, copyright is governed by the Copyright Act of 1976 and is written in the U.S. Code as Title 17. A work must be in a fixed form in order to have copyright. For example, a literary work written on paper or typed in a Microsoft Word file may be copyrighted. A video work captured on film or recorded on a mobile device may also be copyrighted. Content creators hold copyright for their work the moment it is set in a fixed form, and though registering a work with the U.S. Copyright Office provides some benefits, this is not required in order to be afforded copyright protections. The full U.S. copyright law is available online from the U.S. Copyright Office website (https://www.copyright.gov).

The goal of copyright law, as stated in the U.S. Constitution, is to "promote the progress of science and the useful arts" (1787). To accomplish this, the law simultaneously encourages (1) the creation of knowledge by providing content creators exclusive rights to their work, and (2) the reuse of knowledge by allowing some uses by others without needing to obtain permission. This provides an important balance between copyright holders and the furthering of knowledge and creativity by others.

Educators in particular are granted a number of valuable permissions when it comes to using copyrighted material. For instance, Section 110 of Title 17 includes the face-to-face teaching exemption:

Notwithstanding the provisions of section 106, the following are not infringements of copyright:

> (1) performance or display of a work by instructors or pupils in the course of face-to-face teaching activities of a nonprofit educational institution, in a classroom or similar place devoted to instruction, unless, in the case of a motion picture or other audiovisual work, the performance, or the display of individual images, is given by means of a copy that was not lawfully made under this title, and that the person responsible for the performance knew or had reason to believe was not lawfully made;

Thus, in regard to video, the performance (i.e., showing) of films in the classroom without securing permission from the rights holder is lawful as long as conditions such as showing only to students enrolled in the course and using legally obtained copies are in place. Note also that showings may be of films in their entirety, and there is no limitation to a specific medium that must be screened. However, should an instructor wish to show a film outside the classroom (e.g., for a student club event), this generally falls outside the scope of the face-to-face teaching exemption, regardless of whether or not an admission fee is charged. In these cases, securing permission from the copyright owner or purchasing a Public Performance Rights (PPR) license may be required. Some libraries choose to preemptively purchase PPR licenses in anticipation that their video collections will be used in extracurricular activities, while others choose to purchase video content without PPR and focus instead on supporting the curricular activity of their institution. It is helpful for library staff working with streaming video to have an understanding of where their intent lies in this matter, and they have this included in a collection development policy.

TEACH ACT

For the instructional use of copyrighted material outside the traditional classroom, additional copyright exemptions are in place which educators may consult. The Technology, Education and Copyright Harmonization Act, commonly referred to as the TEACH Act, is one such exemption and was created in response to the growth of distance education. Until the TEACH Act was enacted in 2002, copyright law granted a range of uses of copyrighted material in the classroom, but it did not account for the delivery of digital content for online instruction. The TEACH Act amended Section 110(2) to include language relevant to distance education and attempted to align the rights closer to those given to face-to-face teaching.

Unfortunately, the TEACH Act does not provide online instruction with as many permissions as face-to-face teaching enjoys, and it requires a number of conditions to be in place. First, the exemption is limited to a "governmental body or an accredited nonprofit educational institution" to use. The exemption also uses language such as "mediated instructional activities" and "class session," which implies that the use of copyrighted material in online instruction should mirror that of in-person teaching. This, of course, is a challenge because it does not align with one of the key features of online education: asynchronous instruction. Additionally, the TEACH Act requires the instructor's institution to have "policies regarding copyright" in place and to provide "information materials" regarding copyright to its faculty and students. This suggests that an instructor's reliance on the TEACH Act is not a decision made alone but rather with his or her institution, which may be challenging for some without support from the administration. Another challenge with using the TEACH Act is that, unlike the face-to-face teaching exemption, it is meant to be applied only to "reasonable and limited portions" and not to works in their entirety (2002).

Of course, the purpose of the TEACH Act is to allow the use of copyrighted material that an institution has not licensed, so for academic and school libraries that have licensed video content for their student population, the application of copyright exemptions such as the TEACH Act is not necessary. In fact, many streaming vendors encourage instructional use of their videos by offering features such as embed codes for placing content directly into a learning management system. Additionally, if video content already exists online (e.g., YouTube), it is generally considered to be permissible to link to the content. However, one should certainly verify that the content has been uploaded legally before doing so. This can be done by looking for rights and license statements accompanying the video, or by examining the user profile of the person who uploaded it.

Though the TEACH Act was created specifically for distance education, it is not required to use for circumstances related to distance education. For many educators working in online instruction, the scope of the TEACH Act is too limited and its requirements are too complex to adhere to. In these cases, many turn to fair use.

FAIR USE

Fair use is a legal doctrine that permits the limited use and reproduction of copyrighted material in certain circumstances without securing permission from the copyright holder. Its framework is broadly written (a significant difference from the TEACH Act), which allows for a wide array of applications ranging from instruction to commercial ones. Fair use is a valuable right that is intended to promote the use and distribution of knowledge, whether published or unpublished, and it acts as a counterbalance against what would otherwise be a monopoly over the use of copyrighted materials by their owners.

Fair use requires an analysis of the use in question in regard to four factors. These four factors are described in Section 107 of the Copyright Act and are:

(1) the purpose and character of the use, including whether such use is of a commercial nature or is for nonprofit educational purposes;

(2) the nature of the copyrighted work;

(3) the amount and substantiality of the portion used in relation to the copyrighted work as a whole; and

(4) the effect of the use upon the potential market for or value of the copyrighted work.

Due to the case-by-case analyses that it requires, determining fair use can be a time-consuming process. Documenting one's four-factor examination helps to ease this burden. It can also be difficult to determine for one's self or institution whether a use may be deemed fair or not. In cases like these, comparing against defined best practices related to the use or discipline is certainly helpful. Notable best practices related to video, teaching, and libraries include those from the Association of Research Libraries (2012), College Art Association (2015), and the Society for Cinema and Media Studies (2008). Each provides shared understandings and practice for their subject areas that can help shape fair-use determinations and policy.

Many helpful fair-use checklists can be found on the Web, but it is important to understand that a fair-use analysis is not meant to be formulaic. A use deemed fair under one of the four factors does not automatically neutralize an unfair use under another factor. Additionally, a common misconception about fair use is that if a use is for educational purposes, then it is automatically considered fair. This is not true, and a fair-use analysis requires a balanced consideration of all four factors.

COPYRIGHT POLICY

It is important for a library or its educational institution to have a copyright policy in place to guide staff who are making determinations related to copyrighted material. Though copyright law and its exemptions can be clear in some cases, in other cases it is not, and much of it is up to interpretation. Additionally, crafting a copyright policy clarifies an institution's level of risk tolerance, which is useful for determining the appropriate uses of copyrighted materials in more tricky areas. For example, the legality of instructors using personal streaming accounts (e.g., Netflix) in the classroom remains a debated issue. Some educators consider this to fall under fair use or the face-to-face teaching exemption, while others feel that these rights are trumped by the license agreement in place when registering with the service. Having a copyright policy in place helps library staff and educators by providing a shared understanding of how streaming video is approached by one's institution. Since much of copyright and fair use analysis is taken on a case-by-case basis, having a policy also helps to model the thought processes for an institution's staff to follow.

References

Association of Research Libraries. 2012. "Code of Best Practices in Fair Use for Academic and Research Libraries." www.arl.org/storage/documents/publications/code-of-best -practices-fair-use.pdf.

College Art Association. 2015. "Code of Best Practices in Fair Use for the Visual Arts." www.collegeart.org/pdf/fair-use/best-practices-fair-use-visual-arts.pdf.

Society for Cinema and Media Studies. 2008. "Statement of Best Practices for Fair Use in Teaching for Film and Media Educators." *Cinema Journal* 47 (2): 155–64. http:// c.ymcdn.com/sites/www.cmstudies.org/resource/resmgr/fair_use_documents/scms _teaching_statement.pdf.

Technology, Education and Copyright Harmonization Act. 2002. 17 U.S.C. § 110(2).

U.S. Constitution. 1787. Article I, § 8, clause 8.

9

STREAMING VIDEO ACCESSIBILITY

Steven Milewski

According to a 2011 Institute of Education Science report (2008–2009 data), the number of students at two-year and four-year degree-granting postsecondary institutions who had hearing disabilities was approximately 4 percent, and those with visual disabilities numbered approximately 3 percent (Raue and Lewis 2011). While content may drive a library's selection of materials, it is also important to keep accessibility for people with disabilities in mind and to ask questions of the vendors to determine if their content is accessible and to what extent. This reinforces to the vendors that accessibility is an important issue for libraries, colleges, and universities, both for their students and because federal and even state laws are requiring that online instructional videos, including professionally produced education videos, be accessible to people with a wide range of disabilities.

No one disagrees that students with disabilities must be accommodated in all the materials they need for research and coursework, including video materials. There has been some question about how current laws and regulations affect the requirements for accessibility in video streaming as a "just in case requirement," and this area is still a bit vague and is being worked out both in federal and state law and in the courts. Briefly, the Americans with Disabilities Act (ADA) was originally passed in 1990 and was revised in the ADA Amendments Act of 2008 to clarify the intent and interpretations of disability law and to tie the act's language to that of Section 504 of the Rehabilitation Act of 1973 (Department of Education 2012). While there was no direct requirement for universities and colleges to follow Section 504 of the Rehabilitation Act of 1973, this act did add stronger requirements to the ADA. For example, Section 504 makes accessibility a potential civil rights issue. Examples of resulting litigation are the lawsuits brought against MIT and Harvard in 2015 by the National Association for the Deaf for lack of accessibility to video and audio streamed materials (Civil Rights Education and Enforcement Center 2015).

A different section of the Rehabilitation Act of 1973, Section 508, addresses video more than Section 504, especially after its update in 1998. But even though this section only stipulates that federal agencies must follow it, there are many states and agencies that use Section 508 standards for video anyway, because of their own accessibility laws, fear of litigation, and because of federal funding requirements for some programs such as the Assistive Technology Act (Bond 2015). While Section 508 for many years had limited language concerning video, it addressed video more in its revision that came out in January 2017 (United States Access Board 2017). It now has more detailed requirements for audio and video streaming, bringing it even closer to the WCAG 2.0 A and AA guidelines than it had been in the past. WCAG 2.0 (Web Content Accessibility Guidelines) was developed in 2008 by the World Wide Web Consortium's Web Accessibility Initiative. While WCAG 2.0 itself is becoming dated, it has sections on captioning and descriptive audio guidelines for video streaming (World Wide Web Consortium 2008).

CAPTIONING FOR VIDEO

The captioning for video displays the spoken video dialogue as text on the viewing screen and includes a text description of relevant sounds and sound effects. Captions are considered "closed captions" when the viewer is able to turn them on or off as desired, or "open captioned" if the captions are always displayed. Additional captioning selections may also allow captioning to do double duty as a translation feature as well as providing accessibility. Subtitling, while similar, differs in that the text does not include added sound effects and features and does not truly meet accessibility requirements, although it is often better than nothing at all.

The Federal Communications Commission insists on four basic pillars of captioning for television, and these are good basic guidelines for captioning in general.

- *Accurate:* Captions must match the spoken words in the dialogue and convey background noises and other sounds to the fullest extent possible.
- *Synchronous:* Captions must coincide with their corresponding spoken words and sounds to the greatest extent possible and must be displayed on the screen at a speed that can be read by viewers.
- *Complete:* Captions must run from the beginning to the end of the program to the fullest extent possible.
- *Properly placed:* Captions should not block other important visual content on the screen, overlap one another, or run off the edge of the video screen (Federal Communications Commission 2017).

There are three points to make concerning this list. First, background noise and sound effects are important and can convey meaning about events ("distant explosion"), emotions ("eerie music"), and the setting or context ("singing in background"). If the videos do not include such information, then they are simply subtitled. A common example of subtitling is subtitling in foreign language films, the purpose of which is translation more than accessibility. While better than nothing, without these additional descriptions, the captions are not as accessible as they could or should be for the hearing-impaired.

Second, "Properly placed" can be very difficult to achieve for video streaming because of device or player limitations, even though these allow some control over the captions. The vendor Kanopy (https://www.kanopystreaming.com) has excellent caption controls for the user, allowing them to change the caption's text color, text background, font, and font size.

Third, captioning provides universal design benefits for other people besides those with hearing difficulties. For example, for those for whom English is a second language, having captioning can be very useful, allowing them to reinforce the spoken words they hear with the text on the screen, making it easier to comprehend the dialogue of the film. There also can be sections in a video where the audio is very low because of quality or design, or the scene has a lot of background noise, and having captions can help anyone understand the words that are being spoken.

Even with larger vendors, rarely is there captioning for 100 percent of their content, though many vendors are constantly pushing to ensure that new material is accessible and that older material becomes captioned. While there is a recognition of the need for captioning, older videos may not have been captioned or have interactive transcripts, and newer videos are sometimes added to available collections with the intent of adding captions to them later. Many large vendors are receptive to requests from libraries to have particular titles captioned.

INTERACTIVE TRANSCRIPTS

Often, in addition to captioning, a transcript is provided, which is a useful printable and readable text. Many vendors also offer interactive transcripts that offer additional accessibility features. Interactive transcripts are transcripts of the video that appear on one side or below the player window and are displayed synchronously with the audio of the video. This allows someone with hearing difficulties not only to follow the spoken words and sounds, but also to read the dialogue again or to read ahead. Everyone, not just those with hearing disabilities, can do the same, for example, searching for names or terms in the text. Some transcripts enable the user to click on the text and have the video jump to the place that the dialogue is spoken, and enable viewers to watch from there. An additional benefit with some interactive transcripts is that one can turn off the "autoscroll" feature (the ability to scroll around within the interactive transcript) without affecting the video or its captions as it is playing. Also, the interactive transcript can often be printed out as a text copy, or copied and pasted into a word-processing document to be used with a screen reader if desired, although it might not always be perfectly formatted for a screen reader.

AUDIO DESCRIPTION

Audio description is an accessibility feature for people with visual disabilities. It uses an additional audio track separate from the main one that is played at the same time as the regular soundtrack and is also synchronous with the video's timecode. This audio track describes relevant visual information (e.g., colors, facial expressions, etc.) that would not be apparent to someone who could not see the video. For example, an audio description might say "red lava streams down the side of a volcano" during a documentary showing a volcanic eruption. Very few vendors currently have content with audio description.

The Described and Captioned Media Program, or DCMP (https://www .dcmp.org), is a joint effort funded by the U.S. Department of Education and administered by the National Association of the Deaf. It has over 4,000 captioned and described educational media to benefit K–12 students who have visual and/or hearing disabilities. Guidelines for audio description can be found at DCMP's "Description Key" (http://descriptionkey.org/index.html).

KEYBOARD SHORTCUTS AND CONTROLS

Another desirable accessibility feature in a video player or video platform is the ability to control the video using keyboard shortcuts. This allows someone with vision difficulties to control the player without having to see the mouse arrow or "point and click." Using a mouse can also be difficult for people with motor disabilities affecting their hands. While some of these individuals can use the "tab" key to move around the screen, it can be very awkward for them. YouTube's (https://www.youtube.com) player has a good range of keyboard controls. For example, hitting the "j" key allows one to go back ten seconds, while the "l" key lets one jump ahead ten seconds. Very few video vendors offer keyboard controls despite their obvious benefits for people with visual or motor disabilities.

LICENSING

Addressing accessibility features in licensing language is one proactive thing that librarians can do to help their institutions provide accessible video streaming content, especially when licensing the ability to play video material on their institutions' own streaming servers. It is important to ask the campus's legal team to include language allowing the ability to create a captioned version (closed or open captions), audio-described video, and interactive transcripts. Open captioning is not ideal, but sometimes getting caption files off of a DVD that one has licensed to stream can be difficult, and having a separate file with open captions might be the best option. Even though the campus disability services department may have options to create material that is accessible for a registered student with disabilities, the library can be very limited by the license it signs. Librarians should try to get language in the license giving the most flexibility for their institution, including the ability to outsource captioning if necessary. A few examples of this language are given below.

Licensing Examples:

Additional accessible file creation

"University may create an additional DVD or streaming file with open or closed captions or with video descriptions provided that:

No existing captioning exists on the DVD or streaming file or in the case of audio description, no existing audio description exists on the DVD or streaming file"

For fair use

"Copyright Law: For sake of clarity, the parties agree that nothing in this Agreement will limit either party's rights under U.S. copyright law"

ACCESSIBILITY FOR YOUR OWN SERVER/PLAYER

While a lot of video streaming comes from vendors and their servers, there are some videos that can only be licensed for streaming on library or university servers. Often one may be able to get a captioned file with the video streaming file the vendor provides, so one should be sure to ask ahead of time if this is available. If the vendor provides video files and caption files in the library's specified file types, it is also important to check that the timecodes for both are in sync and stay in sync if changing the file type or size. Sometimes one may not be able to get a video file or a caption file, and one will need to create the captions in-house or outsource them. Even being sent the script may help if a vendor has it. Many captioning services will offer reduced pricing if a transcript of the video is provided. The DCMP has a large, though not complete, list of "Caption Service Vendors" at https://www.dcmp.org/ai/10.

CONCLUSION

Video streaming has several unique challenges when it comes to making the material accessible to those with disabilities. Different players may have controls in different areas, interactive text in different locations, and different quality levels of keyboard control, making things confusing for all users, not just those with disabilities. Different types of devices (PCs, workstations, and handheld devices like iPads and smartphones) must all be taken into account when making sure the technology works correctly. Different Internet browsers may display things differently or require certain updates (Flash, for example), and both vendors and libraries must keep those details in mind when trialing and testing. Vendors should be able to describe the accessibility of their material either through a VPAT (Voluntary Product Accessibility Template) or an online statement of accessibility. It is key to ask vendors questions about the different types of accessibility features for the video streaming content they offer. Test the content, test the player on different devices and different browsers, and make sure the license gives the most flexibility concerning accessibility. Most video and video streaming content vendors are working to make their content accessible, but it is important to continue to let them know that accessibility for a wide range of disabilities is an important and often necessary feature for an institution and its students.

References

Bond, Lily. 2015. "How Section 504 and 508 Impact Closed Captioning Requirements." *Blog – 3Play Media*. August 1. www.3playmedia.com/2015/01/08/how-section-504-508-impact-closed-captioning-requirements.

Civil Rights Education and Enforcement Center. 2015. "The National Association of the Deaf et al. v. Harvard, MIT." https://creeclaw.org/online-content-lawsuit-harvard-mit.

Department of Education. 2012. "Questions and Answers on the ADA Amendment Act of 2008 for Students with Disabilities Attending Public and Secondary Schools." https://www2.ed.gov/about/offices/list/ocr/docs/dcl-504faq-201109.html.

Federal Communications Commission. 2017. "Closed Captioning on Television." https://www.fcc.gov/consumers/guides/closed-captioning-television.

Raue, Kimberly, and Laurie Lewis. 2011. "Students with Disabilities at Degree-Granting Postsecondary Institutions." National Center for Education Statistics. https://nces.ed.gov/pubsearch/pubsinfo.asp?pubid=2011018.

United States Access Board. 2017. "Information and Communication Technology (ICT) Final Standards and Guidelines." https://www.access-board.gov/guidelines-and-standards/communications-and-it/about-the-ict-refresh/final-rule.

World Wide Web Consortium. 2008. "Web Content Accessiblity Guidelines (WCAG) 2.0: W3C Recommendation 11 December 2008." https://www.w3.org/TR/WCAG20/-media-equiv.

THE FUTURE

Colin Higgins

We're gonna be in a world a few years from now [in which] the vast majority of content [that] people consume online is going to be video" (Carmichael 2016). So declared Mark Zuckerberg, cofounder and CEO of Facebook, at the World Mobile Congress in 2016. On several occasions, Zuckerberg has maintained that 80 percent of Facebook's content will be video by 2018. His target is both an avowal of ambition and an unexceptional prediction. Facebook Live is already a (sometimes controversial) reality. Instagram—owned by Facebook—has made no secret of its desire to blur the boundaries between photos and videos. Video accounted for 73 percent of all Internet traffic in 2016. According to the technology conglomerate Cisco (2017), this will rise to 82 percent by 2021, with the bandwidth consumed by video rising more than threefold in the same period. Cisco believes that by 2021, "every second, a million minutes of video content will cross the network."

To fans of science fiction, these trends may not be surprising. Video communication has long been a staple of science-fiction literature and film. From the bridge of the Starship *Enterprise*, Captain Picard hailed allies and enemies alike in high-definition video. The ubiquity of video screens in *Blade Runner* was not exactly an accurate prediction—the floating billboards advertised the opportunity to colonize other planets, an opportunity we still await—but it was certainly a prescient one.

Though long-predicted, video streaming is a technology that only entered its maturity less than a decade ago. The wires and modems that connected the first generation of boxy microcomputers to the information superhighway lacked the capacity to stream video. Standard-definition video requires a broadband speed of 2 megabits per second for stable streaming; for high-definition content, a broadband speed of 5 megabits per second is recommended. The dial-up technology through which many of us were first exposed to the Internet in the 1990s had a maximum connection speed of just 56 kilobits per second.

But as Internet connection speeds have increased, so video has grown to become the dominant form of Internet data. And this data is not all cat videos on YouTube and Netflix original programming. By 2014, 40 percent of international telephone traffic took place over Skype (Gara 2014). Video surveillance traffic is growing exponentially. So too is virtual-reality video traffic, in which Facebook is investing heavily. Cisco predicts that virtual-reality video traffic will increase twenty-fold between 2016 and 2021.

In only a decade, video streaming has transformed the way people communicate, learn, procrastinate, and, most obviously, consume entertainment. What might the next decade bring? Making predictions about the future is a dependable way of making oneself look ludicrous. However, several emerging trends are both economically dynamic and conspicuous enough for us to be able to assume their escalating importance. How they will manifest is unclear, but each is likely to have a significant impact on future library services.

First, on-demand video streaming services will continue the steady destruction of traditional television. Between 2011 and 2015, average monthly viewing figures on the Disney, NBC Universal, Time Warner, and Viacom networks fell between 11 and 35 percent. During the same period, the monthly minutes delivered by Netflix grew by 669 percent (Thompson 2017b). Although Americans over age sixty-five are actually watching more television, and there has been a resurgence in cable news, these developments are unlikely to outlive the Trump presidency (Thompson 2017a). The vested interests of slow-moving corporations will ensure that cable and broadcast television will continue into the medium term (*Economist* 2017), and librarians need to be mindful of the siren song of technological determinism. But the days of television, as we used to know it, are surely numbered.

The sales of films on optical discs will also continue to decline as video streaming subscriptions and sales eviscerate the market for DVDs and Blu-ray Discs. In 2016, for the first time, revenues from subscriptions to these services were greater than those from the sale of discs (Wallenstein 2017). There are good reasons for thinking that many people will continue to collect optical discs for some time. They can be given to friends, purchased at supermarket checkouts, displayed on a shelf, and you don't need a subscription to view them. You can borrow them from the library. But there is only so much that people can watch. Increased streaming revenues must inevitably lead to fewer DVDs and Blu-ray Discs being sold.

The best days of television (and perhaps film) production, however, may still be ahead. Upstart Internet firms have a talent for creative destruction. In a decade, Amazon transformed itself from an ambitious online bookshop into one of the world's largest retailers; a decade later, it has become a key player in fields as diverse as robotics, voice recognition, data storage, and commercial drones, not to mention video streaming. Netflix began as a rent-by-mail DVD distribution service; in only a few years it has evolved into a vertically integrated television and motion picture production company.

This transition has parallels with the rise of HBO thirty years ago, and is likely to be just as transformative. For decades, American network broadcasters relied on highly formalized genre conventions, leading to conservative dramas that aimed to sustain market share among mainstream audiences. Relying on subscription-based models, and freed from the constraints of federal regulation, cable television producers took more risks with both content and form. This resulted in radical innovation, with long-form productions like *The Sopranos* (1999–2007), *The Wire* (2002–08), and *Lost* (2004–10) offering complex dramatic arcs, challenging storylines, and idiosyncratic characters.

It is too early to predict how profoundly video streaming will alter television production—*House of Cards*, the first series commissioned by Netflix from its own production arm, was released only in February 2013—though it is clear that the marketplace is evolving. Video streaming services seem to have intensified the trend for what has become known as binge viewing. Since shows are available on-demand by definition, audiences have become more atomized. Writers have developed ever-more complex storylines but, to maintain attention, have also grown dependent on mid-season surprises and end-of-season hooks. Fracturing audiences are leading to the development of hybrid genres. Those fractured audiences themselves are reflected in the social uncertainties of many productions. The data on viewing and purchasing habits mined by Netflix and Amazon have resulted in productions carefully developed for targeted audiences. Many new productions are niche by design.

Some commentators see a flip side to this diversity, and have begun to worry about an emerging "content monopoly." In 2016 Netflix released 30 original scripted television series, received 54 Emmy Award nominations, and spent an estimated $6 billion on programming, producing 126 series, specials, and films (Masters 2016). Netflix now outspends all other American cable and network channels. Concern has been expressed about the company's executive focus which, it is believed, can limit the creative control granted to writers, directors, and producers. Netflix has a financial interest in catering to audience tastes, not challenging them. It creates content, not art. *Vanity Fair* journalist Nick Bilton (2017) has written about his concern that cinema and television may soon be replaced by "digital wallpaper."

However, we are certainly living in an era of unparalleled televisual variety and quality. Television production values and storytelling excellence now rival those of the big screen, with generous budgets drawing the best writers, actors, and directors out of Hollywood. On-demand video streaming did not cause this move away from film, which can be attributed to other factors such as the stranglehold of Hollywood unions, the increasingly global focus of production (leading to the dominance of pyrotechnically abundant superhero movies), and the difficulties involved in financing mid-budget films. But the new opportunities offered by video streaming services have provided a magnet at a fortuitous time.

More recently, video streaming companies have begun to challenge the traditional production and distribution models for motion pictures too. In 2017, *Manchester by the Sea*, distributed by Amazon Studios, received six Academy Award nominations, including one for Best Picture. Though it failed to win in this category, the film received the awards in the Best Actor (for Casey Affleck) and Best Original Screenplay (for Kenneth Lonergan) categories. *The Salesman*, also distributed by Amazon, won the award for Best Foreign Film.

In purchasing the distribution rights for *Manchester by the Sea* for $10 million, Amazon operated like a traditional distribution company—the film received wide theatrical release. A more radical challenge to the economics and culture of film was exposed by the controversy at the Cannes Film Festival in May 2017. Two films financed and distributed by Netflix, *Okja* and *The Meyerowitz Stories*, were shown in competition. Both received excellent reviews, but also generated tortured critical discussion from journalists concerned that the days of cinema as a shared social experience were now numbered.

Netflix has made it clear that it is only interested in distributing films through its video streaming service, not through festivals and theatrical release. Its business model is partly based on its exclusive content. *Okja* and *The Meyerowitz Stories* might be the last films produced by Netflix to be shown at Cannes. In the future, only films with a French theatrical release will be eligible for competition. Netflix-produced films may even be ineligible for the Academy Awards. Films must have at least one week of theatrical showings in Los Angeles and New York to be considered for an Oscar.

Though many in the industry have welcomed the willingness of video streaming services to finance independent films, theatrical releases are still important. When distribution rights for *The Birth of a Nation* were auctioned at the Sundance Film Festival in 2016, Netflix made the highest offer, but a traditional theatrical distributor (Fox Searchlight) won the rights.

The history of the Internet is a history of near-monopolies. However, it is unclear whether Netflix will become the Google of Hollywood, whether Amazon might challenge its rival, whether another company will take their place, or whether the market will remain fractured. Market convergences are still in their infancy, and it is unclear which of these convergences—networks and streaming services, television and film, creator and distributor—will succeed.

What is clear is that no large commercial service is particularly interested in libraries. But as other chapters in this volume have outlined, services are starting to emerge that allow our users to access online video content. Streaming videos have meant that cinema has become less of a shared cultural experience, and more of a private enjoyment. As Nick Bilton (2017) has written, "we will eventually stop going to the movies, which are already expensive, limiting, and inconvenient. Instead the movies will come to us." Librarians are in an excellent position to mediate, facilitate, and inform this access.

The new world brings new responsibilities, and new challenges for our acquisition policies, metadata standards, and indeed our civic responsibilities. How will we make these media available within our libraries? How will we make sure that our poorer, older, younger, and less technically adept users are not disenfranchised by these services? The world of film and television is changing fast. If we still intend to offer our users access to these cultural productions—which I believe we must—we will need to be willing to change just as quickly.

References

Bilton, Nick. 2017. "Why Hollywood as We Know It Is Already Over." *Vanity Fair*, January. www.vanityfair.com/news/2017/01/why-hollywood-as-we-know-it-is-already-over.

Carmichael, Jon. 2016. "Mark Zuckerberg Predicts the Future of the Internet: It's All about VR and Video." *Inverse*. www.inverse.com/article/11853-mark-zuckerberg-predicts-the -future-of-the-internet-it-s-all-about-vr-and-video.

Cisco. 2017. "Cisco Visual Networking Index: Forecast and Methodology, 2016–2021." www .cisco.com/c/en/us/solutions/collateral/service-provider/visual-networking-index-vni/ complete-white-paper-c11-481360.html.

The Economist. 2017. "Traditional TV's Surprising Staying Power." *The Economist*, February 9. www.economist.com/news/special-report/21716459-peak-tv-its-way-slowly-traditional-tvs-surprising-staying-power?frsc=dg%7Cd.

Gara, Tom. 2014. "Skype's Incredible Rise in One Image." *Wall Street Journal*, January 15. http://blogs.wsj.com/digits/2014/01/15/skypes-incredible-rise-in-one-image.

Masters, Kim. 2016. "The Netflix Backlash: Why Hollywood Fears a Content Monopoly." *The Hollywood Reporter*, September 14. www.hollywoodreporter.com/features/netflix -backlash-why-hollywood-fears-928428.

Thompson, Derek. 2017a. "The Donald Trump Show Is Eating Television." *The Atlantic*, April 9. www.theatlantic.com/business/archive/2017/04/the-trump-show/522372.

———. 2017b. "Why the 'End of TV' is Great for Facebook and Google." *The Atlantic*, June 2. www.theatlantic.com/business/archive/2017/06/google-facebook-netflix/528999/.

Wallenstein, Andrew. 2017. "Home Entertainment 2016 Figures: Streaming Eclipses Disc Sales for the First Time." *Variety*, January 6. www.variety.com/2017/digital/news/ home-entertainment-2016-figures-streaming-eclipses-disc-sales-for-the-first -time-1201954154.

ABOUT THE CONTRIBUTORS

John Ballestro is the coordinator of monographic and automated acquisitions at Texas A&M University's Sterling C. Evans Library, where he oversees the acquisition of one-time purchases ranging from monographs to databases, with a focus on e-books and streaming video. His interests include graphic novels and video gaming culture.

Scott Breivold recently reached his thirtieth year as a professional librarian. The majority of his career has been in academic libraries, with a specialization in nonprint media services and collections. In 2017, he served as the interim associate university librarian at California State University, Los Angeles. Breivold is entering his seventeenth year at Cal State LA as the university's media, arts, and web librarian.

Mary Gilbertson is the head of monographs at the University of Arkansas. This position includes supervision of both acquisitions and cataloging. In addition, she is a member of the leadership team that directs collection development. In these roles, she has examined purchasing, processing, and collection development issues, including the study of use statistics, that are related to streaming video.

David Hellman is the collection development coordinator at San Francisco State University, which is part of the California State University system. He was previously a reference librarian and the business subject specialist at Santa Clara University. Hellman is currently involved in all aspects of media acquisitions at his library, and he regularly presents at conferences on a number of collection development topics.

Colin Higgins is the librarian at St. Catharine's College, University of Cambridge. He has research interests in cataloging and classification, and in library history. He is the author of *Cataloging and Managing Film and Video Collections* (2015).

Steven Milewski is an assistant professor at the University of Tennessee, Knoxville, and since 2013 has been the digital media technologies librarian and social work liaison there. He has worked with video-streamed educational media since 2009 and has served as the University Libraries' disability services coordinator since 2013. Milewski chairs the University Libraries' Assistive Technology and Access Committee, is the library representative to the campus's Assistive Technology Implementation Team, and is cochair of the ALA's Video Round Table Program Committee.

Erin DeWitt Miller is the head of the Media Library at the University of North Texas, and in this role she is responsible for managing the UNT Library's streaming video. Formerly, she was the library's electronic resources librarian, and before that she worked as a high school librarian. Her research interests include streaming media, online video usability, and innovative services in academic libraries.

Sue Parks is the associate dean for special libraries at the University of North Texas. Formerly, she was head of the Media Library and worked extensively with streaming video collections and services. She served as president of CCUMC: Leadership in Media & Academic Technology and is actively involved in the ALA, ACRL, and LLAMA.

Peter Shirts is the music librarian in the Heilbrun Music and Media Library at Emory University in Atlanta. He worked previously as the music and audiovisual librarian at the University of Hawaii at Manoa, where he expanded streaming video offerings to meet student and faculty demand and tried to stay ahead in the rapidly changing media environment despite unfavorable budgets.

Andrew Trantham has several years of support staff work experience in public, academic, and academic law libraries, in both access services and technical services. He is currently the electronic resources and contracts assistant for the University of North Texas Libraries, where his primary job duties include reviewing and negotiating the legal language of purchasing contracts. Trantham recently completed his master's degree in library science at the University of North Texas, and he has aspirations to go into library administration in an academic library setting.

Mary Wahl is the digital services librarian at California State University, Northridge, where she works with cataloging, metadata, and streaming media projects. In 2014–2015 she led a team of librarians and staff to identify the challenges of working with streaming video, and then designed and implemented a detailed workflow for video collection development and acquisitions. Wahl holds an MLIS degree from San Jose State University and a BA in film and television from Chapman University.

Wil Weston is currently the head of collections at San Diego State University and is the subject specialist for public affairs, urban studies, and LGBT studies. He earned his doctorate in higher education administration and leadership from the University of New Orleans and his MLIS from Louisiana State University, Baton Rouge. His recent publications include "The Transitioning Library Collection" in *The Generation X Librarian* (2011), and "Revisiting the Tao of Resource Sharing" (2015) in *The Serials Librarian*.

Tim Jiping Zou, an emeritus librarian/professor, was head librarian of the Performing Arts and Media Library at the University of Arkansas, Fayetteville, until his retirement in 2017. He also served as subject librarian for music, theater, dance, film, and Asian studies. His publications cover the areas of library resource-sharing in China, international library resource-sharing, and the cost-effectiveness and models of streaming media resources and service. He was a regular reviewer for *Choice* and served as librarian consultant for the Evergreen Education Foundation.

INDEX